A2 Sociology

Contents

Introduction

■ ■ ■

Content Guidance

■ ■ ■

Questions and Answers

Introduction

About this guide

This unit guide is for students following the OCR A2 Sociology course. It deals with the Module 2539 topic **Social Inequality and Difference**. This topic is designed to give you an understanding of sociological theories, concepts and evidence relating to the underlying processes which shape the life chances of individuals in contemporary Britain. The emphasis is on class, gender and ethnic inequalities in terms of income and wealth, the workplace and poverty. This module is synoptic, which means you will use theories, concepts and evidence about social inequality that you have studied in other units throughout the course, such as the AS units on The Individual and Society, and Culture and Socialisation. Also relevant are the topics covered in the A2 Power and Control unit. This unit also demands some knowledge of the relationship between social inequality, the nature of sociological change, and methods of sociological enquiry.

There are three sections to this guide:
- **Introduction** — this provides advice on how to use this unit guide, an explanation of the skills required in A2 Sociology and suggestions for effective revision. It concludes with guidance on how to succeed in the unit test.
- **Content Guidance** — this provides an outline of what is included in the specification for Social Inequality and Difference. It is designed to make you aware of what you should know before the unit test.
- **Questions and Answers** — this provides mock exam questions on Social Inequality and Difference for you to try, together with some sample answers at grade-A and grade-C level. Examiner's comments are included on how the marks are awarded.

How to use the guide

To use this guide to your best advantage, you should refer to the Introduction and Content Guidance sections from the beginning of your study of Social Inequality and Difference. In order to get full advantage from the Question and Answer section, you would be advised to wait until you have completed your study of the topic, as the questions are wide-ranging. When you are ready to use this section, you should take each question in turn, study it carefully, and either write a full answer yourself or, at the very least, answer parts (a), (b) and (c) fully and write plans for parts (d) and (e). When you have done this, study the grade-A candidate's answer and compare it with your own, paying close attention to the examiner's comments. You could also look at the grade-C answer and, using the examiner's comments as a guide, work out how to rewrite it to gain higher marks.

Learning Centre / Canolfan Dysgu
Coleg y Cymoedd
Aberdare Campus
Tel: 01685 887510

The A2 specification

The aims of the OCR A2 Sociology specification are:

- to develop in you an applied sociological knowledge and understanding of the concepts underpinning contemporary social processes and structures that are relevant to your social identity and your experiences of the social world in the twenty-first century
- to equip you with an in-depth theoretical awareness of how sociological perspectives explain the world you live in and how these interact to provide an integrated set of ideas about how society operates
- to examine how sociologists go about collecting information about the social world in which you live and whether their views on how your everyday world is organised are truthful and worthwhile
- to equip you with the necessary skills to engage in sociological debate, especially in terms of being able to interpret, apply and evaluate relevant evidence and to construct convincing sociological arguments
- to develop in you an appreciation and understanding that sociology is an interconnected academic discipline that requires you to make links between different topic areas, especially with regard to inequality and difference, and methods of sociological enquiry.

Examinable skills

There are three main examinable skills in the A2 specifications, divided into two **Assessment Objectives**.

Assessment Objective 1

Assessment Objective 1 (AO1) is **knowledge and understanding**, which accounts for 46% of A2 marks on offer. Grade A candidates are expected to demonstrate a wide-ranging and detailed knowledge of relevant sociological theories, concepts, methods and different types of evidence, especially statistical data and empirical studies. You will also need to demonstrate a holistic understanding of how different areas are related to the topic of social inequality and difference.

It is important that your acquisition of knowledge goes beyond learning by rote — you also need to demonstrate a clear understanding of what you are describing. In other words, you will be expected to discuss or debate the merits of particular arguments in an organised fashion. This involves learning and using knowledge which is appropriate and relevant to the question set. A good way of doing this is to ask yourself the following questions:

- Do I know the main arguments in the area I am studying?
- Do I know the main sociologists who have contributed to debate in this area?

- Do I know the historical context in which these sociologists are writing?
- Do I understand the concepts used by these sociologists?
- Do I know the empirical studies and data that can be used as evidence to support or undermine particular sociological arguments?

Assessment Objective 2

Assessment Objective 2 (AO2) is broken down into **AO2 (a) interpretation and analysis**, which is worth 27% of the A2 marks on offer, and **AO2 (b) evaluation**, which is also worth 27% of the A2 marks.

Interpretation and analysis essentially involves showing the ability to select and analyse different types of evidence and data. In particular, it involves the ability to address the specifics of the question that has been set by applying and linking socio-logical evidence to specific sociological arguments or theory. It also involves the ability to interpret quantitative and qualitative data, i.e. to work out what the data are saying and/or to put them into your own words. It is useful to ask yourself the following questions when working out whether you have acquired this skill:

- What knowledge in the form of studies, concepts etc. is relevant when addressing a particular debate?
- Can I distinguish between facts and opinions?
- Am I capable of identifying patterns and trends in sociological data and uncover-ing hidden meanings?
- Am I addressing the question throughout the response?
- Am I using the data and information that the examiners have given to me in the items to full effect?
- Have I applied contemporary issues and debates to the question?
- What evidence in the form of sociological studies and statistical data can I use to support or criticise particular arguments?
- Have I put too much of my personal opinion into my response?

Evaluation normally involves assessing the validity of particular sociological arguments and available evidence and data in a balanced way. Critically examining the reliability of the methods used to collect evidence is also very important. The skill of evaluation is an essential one, and should be applied to all the material you come across during your study of the topic. It is useful to ask yourself the following questions when practising this skill:

- How many sides to the debate can be identified in this topic area?
- How was the evidence gathered?
- Can the evidence be checked?
- Is there any other evidence relating to this?
- Is the research relevant to contemporary society?
- Who does not agree with this view and why?
- Which evidence and arguments are most convincing and why?
- What have particular sociologists got to gain from saying what they do?
- Are class, gender and ethnicity taken into account?

In more practical terms, evaluation means that whenever you are introduced to a sociological perspective or study, you should find and learn at least three criticisms that have been made of it. It is important to understand that evaluation can be made up of specific criticisms of a particular theory and its supporting evidence or its methods of data collection, and/or alternative theories which can be used as a point of contrast. However, you will need to be flexible. Do not merely apply all the criticism you have learned to the debate. Be willing to adapt it so that it makes sense according to the sociological context.

Study skills and revision strategies

Good preparation for revision starts the minute you begin to study sociology. One of the most important revision aids that you will have is your sociology folder, so it is important that you keep this in good order. Go back over your essays and exam answers, read your teacher's comments, and use these to see whether you can redo any pieces that did not score particularly good marks.

You should always write down the definition of a concept when you first come across it — use a separate part of your folder for this. In addition, it is useful to make a brief summary of research studies, particularly those not found in your textbook. Remember to include the title, author(s) and, most importantly, the date along with your summary of the method(s) used and the main findings. These should be kept in a section in your sociology folder, or you may wish to record them on a set of index cards.

Another important aspect of revision is to practise writing answers within the appropriate time limit. Make sure you have sufficient time not only to complete all the parts of the question, but also to reread your answer, in order to correct any silly mistakes that may have crept in while working under pressure.

Finally, you need to ensure that you have a thorough understanding of a range of appropriate theories, concepts and studies. Comprehensive revision is not something that can be done the night before the exam — you should start at least 3 weeks before. Construct a revision timetable in order to plan your topics. One way would be to aim to do 90 minutes an evening from Monday to Thursday, take Friday night off, and do 3 hours of revision over the weekend. It is a good idea to revise in concentrated bursts of time. People differ in this respect, but it is seldom a good idea to spend more than 1 hour on revision without a break. Reward yourself: revise for an hour and then watch a television programme, have a snack or listen to some music. Vary your revision programme, too. You could, for example, spend 45 minutes revising Social Inequality and Difference, and then another 45 minutes revising some aspect of Power and Control which has a synoptic link to Social Inequality and Difference. The weekend revision session should involve setting aside some time to have a go at a question under timed conditions. It is important that you practise recall under timed conditions as much as possible.

The unit test

Social Inequality and Difference is the only Module 2539 topic, and the unit examination will contain a choice of two data-response questions. You will have to answer one of these in 90 minutes. The unit as a whole is worth 20% of the full A-level. Each data-response question totals 90 marks, composed of 42 marks for AO1 (knowledge and understanding), 24 marks for AO2a (interpretation and analysis) and 24 marks for AO2b (evaluation).

Each question in the examination will contain two **items** of source material, Item A and Item B. The items are designed to assist your understanding of the area of the unit being examined. One of these items is likely to be made up of text, while the other is likely to be statistical in nature, i.e. in the form of a table or graph. It is essential that you spend some time carefully reading through these items, especially as some of their content will give you clues as to the direction your responses might take and some should be actively used in your response. Each question is broken down into a number of parts, (a) to (e), each with its own mark allocation.

Part (a) is worth **6 marks** and will use the command word **identify** in order to test the skill of interpretation and analysis. You will be asked to examine either Item A or B and to identify **two** things from the textual or statistical data. These could be trends, patterns, characteristics, features etc. The answer to this question is in the data and therefore you should not offer any extra information. A common error is that candidates offer explanations for trends and so on — do not be tempted to do this. You will not be rewarded and you will have wasted valuable time and effort. If the data are statistical, make sure you have a clear idea of how they are organised in terms of scale, proportion, over time etc. A common way of losing marks is not to read statistical data properly. Do make sure too that you distinguish clearly between the two things you are asked to identify. It is a good idea to number them. You should spend approximately 5 minutes on this question.

Part (b) is also worth **6 marks** and will also use the command word **identify** in order to test the skill of interpretation and analysis. You will be asked to examine Item A or B and identify **two** things from the data, i.e. trends, patterns, characteristics, features etc. Again, the answer is in the data and you should not be tempted to offer more than is being asked for. Follow the same advice as for part (a) above with regard to statistical data, to distinguish clearly between the two things in question, and on timing.

Part (c) is **synoptic**, and you should be ready to apply your knowledge of sociological research methods to answering this question. It is worth **12 marks**, all of which are aimed at testing your interpretation and analysis skills. You should pay special attention to the context of the question, i.e. is it on poverty, or social class, or race? Make sure your response is firmly focused on and linked to the specific problem identified in the question. The question will always use the command phrase **identify and explain**, and will be concerned with **two** things connected to research methods and some aspect of social inequality and difference. There are a number of possible varia-tions in the question. For example, questions may focus on:

- two problems in collecting data on an aspect of inequality, such as wealth or poverty
- two problems or difficulties in operationalising a social inequality and difference concept such as social class
- two strengths or two weaknesses of using a particular research method in inves-tigating some aspect of social inequality and difference
- one strength and one weakness of using a particular research method in investi-gating some aspect of social inequality and difference

You should be aware that the question may focus on both primary and secondary types of research methods. Make sure that you distinguish between the two things identified. The command word **explain** means that you should add a brief paragraph that explains the difficulty, weakness, strength etc. How has it come about, and why is it important? Illustrate it with examples if you can. You should spend about 10 minutes on this question.

Part (d) is also **synoptic** and will focus on how the evidence from sociological studies or secondary data (such as official statistics) supports particular debates relating to workplace inequalities, poverty or more general inequalities relating to social class, gender and ethnicity. This evidence may be taken from what you have learned specif-ically as part of the Social Inequality and Difference module, but it should be supple-mented by evidence from other units. These might be from your AS units or from the Power and Control topic you will have studied at A2. It is very important that when you revise for this question you build up a 'synoptic store' of evidence that can be used to support the view in the question.

Part (d) is worth **22 marks**, and the skill rewarded is knowledge and understanding. The question will read 'using your wider sociological knowledge, outline the evidence' or 'identify how something (e.g. social class inequalities) affects something else (e.g. life chances)'. Note that this question asks you to carry out four distinct but interrelated tasks.

(1) 'Using your wider sociological knowledge' means using material from other topic areas (you can also use material from the Social Inequality and Difference module).

(2) The command word 'outline' means you have to summarise or describe that material. You do not have to explain it or evaluate it.

(3) The emphasis is on 'evidence'. It is important that you can distinguish between abstract theory and empirical evidence gathered through research. The latter is much more likely to be rewarded than the former. Evidence may be composed of sociological studies or statistical data that confirm particular patterns and trends.

(4) The question is likely to ask you to outline the evidence in support of a particular view, e.g. that 'social class is still an important influence on life chances in the contemporary UK' or to show 'how' evidence supports a particular view, e.g. 'how patriarchy affects opportunities in the workplace for women'. There are no marks for evaluation, so there is no need to show opposing or challenging evidence.

You should spend approximately 20 minutes answering this question, and aim to fill about two sides of your answer book.

Part (e) is worth 44 marks. It is an essay question which will use the command words **outline and assess**. It will ask you to outline and assess sociological explanations or theories relating to general theories of social stratification (i.e. the hierarchical organisation of UK society in regard to social class, gender/patriarchy and race/ethnicity), workplace inequality and poverty. It aims to test two skills: there are 20 marks for knowledge and understanding, and 24 marks for evaluation.

It is important that you develop the skill of writing essays under timed conditions. It is a good idea to begin your essay by constructing an introduction that sets the scene. This should aim to explain the point of view contained in the question, to define any technical terms used in the question and to identify the key players in terms of sociologists or theories involved in the debate. You should then explain the view embodied in the question by outlining the key features of particular sociological positions. It is sometimes useful to do this by first outlining the theoretical argument(s) and then supporting these with empirical sociological studies or statistical data. What is important throughout this stage is that you clearly link whatever you are discussing to the view contained in the question. Once you have outlined and supported the view contained in the question, you can address the evaluation of that view. Note that more marks are allocated to this skill, so your critical appraisal must be fairly substantial. You may like to begin by addressing specific features of the theories/studies/data already discussed which you think are problematic. The key here is to make sure that the examiner knows you are engaged in evaluation, so use evaluative words or phrases to draw attention to this, e.g. 'however'. Once you have finished with the specifics, you should outline any alternative theories (with supporting evidence) that challenge the view in the question. Do make sure, however, that you clearly state *how* the alternative set of theories challenges the previous position. A common error is to forget to do this.

Finally, try to end with some sort of conclusion. There are two types. You may go for a summative conclusion, which merely reminds the examiner of the competing positions and how they generally differ. But you may prefer an evaluative conclusion, in which you make a judgement based on the evidence as to which position has more validity as a convincing argument. You should aim to spend 40 minutes on this question and to fill at least four sides of your answer book.

Content
Guidance

This section is intended to show you the major issues and themes covered in **Social Inequality and Difference**. However, it is not an exhaustive or comprehensive list of the concepts, issues and sociological studies that you could use to answer questions on this topic. Rather, it is an outline of the key concepts that you need to know plus guidance on some issues and sociological studies that are worth further investigation. You should be able to access further information by consulting your teacher, and by using your textbook and past copies of *Sociology Review*.

The content of **Social Inequality and Difference** falls into three main areas:
- **the dimensions of workplace inequality**
- **poverty as a dimension of inequality**
- **explanations of inequality and difference**

The topic is designed to give you an understanding of the underlying processes which shape the life chances and social identities of specific social groups, and in particular the inequality that tends to characterise relationships between different social classes, between men and women, and between ethnic groups. It also examines how these inequalities might be related to and even caused by the social organisation of contemporary Britain. It is therefore important that we examine wider structural influences, such as the nature of work in modern societies, globalisation, the changing class structure, culture, patriarchy and institutional racism, to understand the constraints that impact on individual social action, especially in regard to poverty, wealth and life chances in education and health.

Defining stratification and concepts of class

You should be aware of three key aspects of the Social Inequality and Difference unit when you start revising and start to use the information below. First, it is important to become familiar with, and be able to apply accurately, the concepts and theories that underpin the central topic areas in this unit, and to support them, whenever possible, with empirical sociological studies. Particularly, you need to have a detailed knowledge and understanding of theory. Second, it is important to develop evaluative understanding of concepts, theories and studies. Evaluation as a skill is highly rewarded at this level. Third, it is important to have a 'synoptic awareness', that is, to know how evidence from other topic areas across both the AS and A2 units might be used to support the view that class, gender and ethnic inequalities exist.

Social stratification

- Social stratification means the division of society into a pattern of layers or strata made up of a hierarchy of unequal social groups.
- In societies characterised by stratification, normally one or two groups dominate the others, and these societies consequently contain inequalities in factors such as wealth and income, occupation and status, social class, political power, religion, race, gender and age.
- Sociologists have identified **four types of stratification systems** which have existed throughout history, some of which are still around today. These are the caste system, the feudal estate system, the apartheid system, and social class.
- The social stratification system found in modern industrial societies, such as the UK, is based on social class.

Concepts of class

- Social classes are groups of people who share a similar economic position through occupation, income and ownership of wealth, as well as having similar levels of education, status, lifestyle (i.e. living standards) and power.
- Class systems are not based on religion or law or race, but on economic factors such as jobs and money.
- In class systems there is no clear distinction between classes. For example, it is difficult to say where the working class ends and the middle class begins.
- All members of societies with class systems, whether working or middle or upper classes, enjoy equal rights.

- There are no legal restrictions on marriage between members of different social groups in societies characterised by class.
- Class societies are open societies in that people can experience downward or upward social mobility, i.e. they can move up or down the class structure through jobs, the acquisition of wealth or marriage.
- Class systems are usually meritocratic, i.e. people are not born into ascribed roles but are encouraged to better themselves through achievement at school, and at work through working hard and gaining promotion.

Defining and measuring social class

- Occupation is the most common measure of social class used by governments, by advertising agencies doing market research, and by sociologists when undertaking social surveys.
- Occupation is generally a good guide to people's skills and qualifications, their income, their future prospects and their present standard of living.
- Occupation usually shapes status in modern society, i.e. most people judge their social standing and that of others by the jobs they do.

The Registrar-General's scale of occupations

- The Registrar-General's (RG) Scale was used to categorise people into social classes in the UK by the government until 2000.
- The RG scale divided the population into five broad social classes:
  - **Class I:** Professional, e.g. accountants, doctors, solicitors.
  - **Class II:** Intermediate, e.g. teachers, managers, pilots, farmers.
  - **Class III NM:** Skilled non-manual, e.g. office workers, shop assistants.
  - **Class III M:** Skilled manual, e.g. electricians, plumbers, factory foremen.
  - **Class IV:** Semi-skilled manual, e.g. agricultural workers, postal workers.
  - **Class V:** Unskilled manual, e.g. road-sweepers, labourers, refuse collectors.
- Classes I, II and III NM were categorised as middle class, and workers in these categories included professionals, managers and white-collar workers.
- Classes III M, IV and V were categorised as working class, and workers in these categories were referred to as blue-collar workers.
- The RG scale was used from 1911 and therefore allowed comparisons over time.

Evaluation
  - The RG scale excluded members of the wealthy upper class who own property and have a great deal of power but who often don't have an occupation, because they live off rents and stocks and shares.

- Groups outside paid employment were excluded, such as housewives and the never-employed/unemployed.
- Classifying unemployed people on the basis of their last job assumed that they had the same income, status, lifestyle etc., but this is unlikely to be the case.
- The RG scale focused on the job of the 'head of the household', and this is generally assumed to be the man. Married women therefore were classified on the basis of their husbands' occupations rather than their own, which was a dated and sexist approach considering the number of married women who now go out to work.
- The focus on the head of the household neglected those families in which both partners are important in bringing home a wage (dual-career families). Their joint incomes could give them the lifestyle of a higher class.
- Some sociologists have suggested that the RG scale was dated because it did not consider cross-class families in which the female has a higher-paid job and status than the male.
- The RG scale failed to consider the increasing number of single working women and single working mothers, because it determined their social class with reference to fathers or ex-husbands.
- There are major differences between occupations within the social classes, especially in terms of income. For example, Social Class I included doctors but this group encompassed highly paid surgeons and poorly paid junior doctors.

Key concepts

stratification; caste system; feudalism; apartheid; social class; social mobility; meritocratic; ascribed and achieved roles; status; working class; middle class

The National Statistics–Socioeconomic Classification (NS–SEC)

- In 2000, the RG scale was replaced by the National Statistics–Socioeconomic Classification (NS–SEC) devised by John Goldthorpe. This is also based on employment.
- The RG scale was abandoned because it failed to reflect the massive decline in manufacturing, the huge growth in service industries (finance and retail) and the large increase in the proportion of women in the workforce.
- The NS–SEC is based on data from the Labour Force Survey on the employment conditions of over 65,000 individuals across 371 occupations.
- It differs from the RG scale in that it is no longer based purely on skill.
- It is based on (a) employment relations, i.e. whether people are employers, self-employed, employed, whether they exercise authority etc., and (b) employment or market conditions, i.e. salary scales, promotion prospects, sick pay, how much control people have over hours worked or how work is done.

- The NS–SEC recognises eight social classes rather than five.
  - **(1)** Higher managerial and professional occupations
  - **(2)** Lower managerial and professional occupations
  - **(3)** Intermediate occupations
  - **(4)** Small employers and own-account workers
  - **(5)** Lower supervisory, craft and related occupations
  - **(6)** Semi-routine occupations
  - **(7)** Routine occupations
  - **(8)** Long-term unemployed or the never-worked
- The NS–SEC no longer divides workers along manual and non-manual lines. Each category contains both manual and non-manual workers.
- Class 8 is essentially the 'underclass', which the RG scale did not cater for because of the emphasis on occupation.
- Occupations such as check-out assistants and sales assistants, who used to be in Class III NM, have been dropped to Class 6 because of their relatively poor conditions of employment (their market situation has deteriorated in terms of pay, job security, autonomy etc.).
- Teachers have been promoted from Social Class II to Class 1, higher professionals, because their market position has improved in terms of pay etc.
- The self-employed are recognised as a separate category.
- Women are recognised as a distinct group of wage earners and are no longer categorised according to the occupations of their husbands or fathers.

Evaluation

- The NS-SEC classification is still primarily based on occupation, and this may differ from people's subjective interpretation of their class position.
- The NS–SEC has taken into consideration changing class boundaries, e.g. the fact that the social position of clerical workers has declined, but there are still significant differences within categories between occupations. For example, do teachers really share the same market position as lawyers and doctors?
- The NS–SEC tells us very little about the huge differences within occupations, e.g. GPs and junior doctors are paid considerably less than consultants.
- It still fails to account for those wealthy enough not to have to work.

Key concepts

employment relations; market conditions; underclass

The dimensions of workplace inequality

Contemporary changes in the distribution of income and wealth

A number of observations can be made concerning the distribution of income and wealth between 1945 and 1997.
- Between 1979 and 1997, income inequality between the rich and poor widened until it was at its greatest since records began at the end of the nineteenth century. This was because the top rate of income tax was lowered, VAT increased from 8% to 17.5%, and there were large salary rises for 'fat-cat' business leaders.
- Between 1979 and 1992, average income rose by 36%, but it rose by 62% for the top 10% of earners, while it fell by 17% for the poorest 10% of earners.
- The level of inequality in income rose faster in the UK than in any other Western nation.
- Overall, the twentieth century saw a gradual redistribution of wealth in the UK. In 1911 the richest 1% of the population owned 69% of the wealth, but this had fallen to 18% by 1991.
- The redistribution of wealth was very narrow — from the very wealthy (the top 1%) to the wealthy (the top 10%), i.e. to family members in order to avoid paying death duties.
- Inheritance was still an important source of wealth, e.g. Harbury and Hitchens (1979) found that 36% of those in the top 0.1% of the wealthy had inherited their wealth in 1973.
- John Scott points out that the richest 1% of the population own 75% of all privately owned shares.

Evaluation
- As wealth takes many different forms, such as stocks and shares, capital in banks and building societies, property such as land, housing, cars, antiques and paintings, it is difficult to estimate.
- Abercrombie and Warde note that wealth is more concealed than income.
- The wealthy tend to redistribute their assets to family members before they die.
- Survey research is not very effective in this area because personal wealth is regarded as a personal and private matter.

Income: the work of Will Hutton
- The 30–30–40 thesis of Will Hutton (1995) suggests that the UK has become split into segments based on inequalities in income and wealth.

- The bottom 30% are the disadvantaged, i.e. the unemployed and those in poverty.
- The second 30% are marginalised, insecure and low-paid workers, including the growing army of part-timers and casual workers (of whom 80% are women), and the increasing number of self-employed.
- The top 40% are the privileged who have held full-time jobs or been self-employed for more than 2 years.

Key concepts

redistribution of wealth; inequality; 30–30–40 thesis; poverty

Contemporary workplace inequalities

Class

- The Low Pay Unit argues that low pay is the most important cause of poverty.
- 45% of British workers are earning less than two thirds of the average hourly wage.
- Low-paid workers are often caught in a poverty trap, i.e. they earn above the minimum level required to claim benefits, but the deduction of tax etc. takes them below it.
- Low pay also results from the weakening of workers' legal rights and high levels of unemployment, although New Labour introduced a minimum wage policy in 1999.

Gender

- Since the 1950s there has been a trend towards the feminisation of the labour force. Between 1969 and 1989 the number of female workers in the UK rose by 2.25 million.
- 48% of the UK labour force is female.
- The UK labour market is characterised by horizontal segregation, meaning that different sectors of employment are dominated by either male or female workers — primary school teaching is overwhelmingly female, whereas higher education is a male preserve with only about 25% of jobs filled by women.
- The UK labour market is also characterised by vertical segregation, meaning that males and females dominate different levels of jobs in terms of status, skill and pay.
- Women tend to be concentrated at lower levels in terms of skill and status, and often encounter the 'glass ceiling', i.e. they are denied access to upper professional and management jobs.
- The Equal Opportunities Commission (EOC) noted in 2001 that only 17% of all professionals, 31% of all managers and 5% of all company directors are female.
- A gender pay gap exists. The EOC estimates that the average pay gap between men and women has remained steady at 20%.
- Women are more likely than men to be employed in part-time work and in temporary or casual labour.

- Male unemployment is higher than female unemployment, although this is due to the gender bias of official statistics, which do not recognise housewives as available for work.

Evaluation
- There is some evidence that horizontal segregation may be in decline because of the general decline in male employment.
- Recent female trends in educational success may also undermine the horizontal labour market.
- Movement of men into female-dominated areas like nursing may have negative implications for women in terms of vertical segregation.
- Hakim argues that the feminisation of the labour force is exaggerated because most of the increase is in part-time rather than full-time work.
- Official female unemployment rates are rising faster than male unemployment rates.

Ethnicity

- Unemployment rates for white men were 8% in 1995 compared with 18% for Pakistani/Bangladeshi men and 21% for black (African-Caribbean) men.
- Unemployment is particularly severe for young ethnic minority people. In 1995 unemployment among young whites aged 16–24 was 17%, but it was 36% for African-Caribbean youth and 33% for Pakistani/Bangladeshi youth.
- In 1995 Ouseley estimated that 62% of young black males in London were unemployed.
- There is evidence of racial discrimination in the job market. Research by Brown and the 'Black and White' television documentary set in Leeds in 1998 showed employers turning away black applicants saying that jobs had gone, but offering interviews to white candidates who turned up later.
- In 1995–96 ethnic minority groups as a whole were more likely to be in management and administration than other types of work. For example, 52% of Indians, 38% of Pakistanis and Bangladeshis and 46% of African-Caribbeans were employed in this sector compared with 51% of whites.
- In 1995–96 equal proportions of white people and people from ethnic minorities worked in manufacturing, but larger proportions of ethnic minorities than whites worked in retail, health and social work.
- Ethnic minorities generally earn lower incomes compared with the majority ethnic population. In 1995 average hourly earnings of full-time employees from ethnic minorities were about 92% of those of white employees.

Key concepts
poverty trap; feminisation of labour force; horizontal segregation; vertical segregation; glass ceiling; gender pay gap; ethnicity; racial discrimination

The impact of changes in the workplace on class, gender and ethnic inequality

The changing nature of the economy

The occupational structure (the organisation of work into full-time employed, part-time employed, unemployed and so on, as well as categories of skill and authority, such as professional, managerial, white-collar, skilled, semi-skilled and unskilled manual work) has changed over time. A number of trends can be seen.

- Between 1986 and 1997, the number of people in jobs rose from 26.9 million to 27.9 million, because more women entered the labour market.
- The primary sector (e.g. heavy industries such as coal-mining, iron and steel, shipbuilding) and the secondary sector (e.g. manufacturing or factory work) of the economy have both gone into decline because of worldwide recession and globalisation — the same raw materials and goods can be produced more cheaply in the developing world.
- Male manual work has consequently gone into decline.
- The tertiary or service sector of the economy (mainly focused around personal services, state services, such as education and welfare, and retail and finance) has expanded in the past 20 years because mass secondary education and the expansion of both further and higher education have ensured the existence of a well-educated and qualified workforce.
- In 1951 only 4% of workers were part-time, but this had increased to 25% by 1993, and by 1996, 85% of part-time jobs were held by women.
- There has been a movement towards the casualisation of the labour force, e.g. there has been an increase in non-standard contracts. Just under one third of employees in the late 1990s were part-time or temporary.
- The deterioration of the labour market has had a severe effect upon men, especially young men, who are now more likely to be unemployed and less likely to be in continuous, long-term and stable work.
- In 1999 the Joseph Rowntree Foundation found that from the mid-1990s the greatest increase in job insecurity occurred among non-manual workers, although the study concluded that this was subjective insecurity rather than due to a real threat.
- Some sociologists argue that the idea of 'a job for life' will soon be a thing of the past.
- Some sociologists predict the emergence of 'portfolio workers', people who will have a 'skills portfolio' — a number of different job skills and credentials, which they will use to move between jobs throughout their working lives.

The impact of globalisation

- The search for new markets encourages the expansion of companies and causes the division of labour under capitalism to become more international. Employment

content guidance

in the UK is increasingly affected by decisions taken by companies that have their headquarters in another country.

- Many transnational companies are 'multi-plant' companies — different parts of products are manufactured across an international division of labour, i.e. in factories across the world, and they are assembled in less economically developed countries.
- Transnational employment may be insecure as such companies are driven to cut costs, especially labour. Raleigh, the bicycle manufacturer, closed its factories in the UK and now manufactures in the Far East, because overheads in the form of wages are cheaper.
- Transnationals may be tempted to close operations in the UK because less economically developed nations can offer them tax advantages, restrictions on trade union activity, and so on.
- Ritzer developed the idea of McDonaldisation, where global companies develop networks of technologies, skills, brands etc. to ensure that in every country more or less the same product is manufactured and delivered in the same way.
- McDonaldisation may result in new kinds of low-skilled, low-paid, standardised jobs for young people (McJobs).

Key concepts

new international division of labour; transnationals; McDonaldisation

Industrial or postindustrial society?

Some sociologists have concluded that changes in the economy and in patterns of employment mean that the UK has moved from being an industrial society to a postindustrial society. Industrial society is characterised by:

- an emphasis on the industrial production of goods in factories
- Fordism, i.e. a form of mass manufacturing production based on assembly lines (as symbolised by those used in Ford's car factories) producing standardised products
- work on assembly lines, fragmented into small tasks that can be carried out repeatedly by semi-skilled labour, relatively cheaply — workers are deskilled
- alienated factory workers — the jobs do not produce job satisfaction, or allow workers much control or autonomy
- control of the labour process and speed of the assembly line by a centralised, hierarchical management, which is sometimes in conflict with the unions that represent the labour force

Postindustrial society is characterised by:

- an emphasis on the provision of services, especially those involved in the processing of knowledge and information — postindustrial society is an 'information society'
- a deindustrialisation of society — manual work in large factories is being replaced by robot technology and computers

- post-Fordism, a form of flexible and diverse small-scale production based on responding quickly to changes in consumption and demand
- work having 'functional flexibility' (i.e. the multi-skilled worker can perform a variety of jobs) and 'numerical flexibility' (i.e. the number of full-time secure workers, part-timers and temporary or casual workers depends on market demand for products and services)
- full-time workers having greater skill (being multi-skilled), being more adaptable and flexible, more highly trained (they have experienced 'upskilling'), and being more motivated and committed
- industrial relations proceeding by consensus and cooperation rather than conflict, because management–worker relations are less hierarchical and are based on common goals

Evaluation

- The case for deindustrialisation has been overstated. Manufacturing still makes up a significant part of the economy and employs a major part of the workforce.
- The service sector has been subjected to industrial principles, e.g. the fast food sector is organised along Fordist lines.
- Information and knowledge have always underpinned industrialisation.
- The service sector has been steadily increasing in size since the industrial revolution.
- Mass production has always been flexible and adaptable, and has always employed the so-called post-Fordist techniques of functional and numerical flexibility.
- Modern work is not about increasing workers' skills but about increasing their workload, i.e. it is multi-tasking rather than multi-skilling.
- Upskilling has only been experienced by professionals, managers and a skilled minority.
- Semi-skilled and unskilled workers have become economically less secure because of the employment of more part-time female workers, temporary or casual workers and the contracting out of some work to agencies.
- Marxists point out that so-called post-Fordist techniques are merely new tools invented by capitalism — managers still control the labour process on behalf of owners and shareholders (i.e. the capitalist class), and pay and conditions of service generally depend on the need to produce goods and services as cheaply as possible so the greatest amount of profit is made.

Key concepts

casualisation; globalisation; tertiary/service sector; postindustrial society; deskilling; alienation; autonomy; information society; deindustrialisation; post-Fordism; functional flexibility; multi-skilling; upskilling; consensus

Workplace change and its impact on class formation and identity

The upper class

- A strong and healthy upper class continues to exist in the UK.
- Over the course of the century, the upper class has changed its character from being predominantly landed gentry and aristocracy to merge with new wealth based on manufacturing, retail and finance.
- Scott argues that the upper class is a 'unified property class' which owns and controls major sections of the manufacturing, financial (e.g. banks) and retail (e.g. supermarkets) sectors.
- Scott notes that the upper class or 'establishment' permeate top positions in politics, the civil service, the Church, the armed services and the professions, especially law.
- The traditional aspects of upper-class culture remain undisturbed, especially the importance of the public schools, the old-boy network, intermarriage and therefore social closure. Mobility into this group is therefore largely restricted.
- Adonis and Pollard (1998) suggest that the upper class has been supplemented by a 'super class' comprising those who have made their fortunes in the City, accountants and managers of investment funds and directors of the former public utilities (water, gas, electricity, British Rail).
- Members of this super class tend to intermarry, earn combined super-salaries, and are distinguished from the rest of society by consumption patterns which revolve around nannies and servants, second homes, exotic holidays and modern art, private health and pension schemes and private education for their children.
- Most of the super class live in London and the southeast.

The middle classes

In 1911 80% of workers were in manual occupations (working-class positions). This number fell to 52% in 1981 and to 32.7% in 1991. In the past 10 years, non-manual workers (traditionally seen as middle class) have become the majority occupational group in the workforce. Savage (1995) notes that in 1991, 29.4% of the workforce worked in the professions and management, 10.7% were self-employed and 27.2% were routine white-collar workers. In other words, 67.3% of the working population could be considered as part of the middle class. He argues that it is important to see that the middle class divides into 4 'class fractions'.

The self-employed or 'petit-bourgeoisie'

- This group makes up 10% of the workforce.
- The number of managers who prefer to work for themselves, for example as consultants, rose considerably in the 1980s, especially in the finance and computer industries.

- Some writers argue that many firms now prefer to contract services to outside consultants rather than employ people themselves.
- A large number of people, again mainly managers, have businesses on the side while continuing to be employees.
- There are some signs that members of this group of workers, who have traditionally been both conservative and passive in pursuit of their interests, are becoming more militant.

Professionals

- Savage et al. argue that higher and lower professionals mainly recruit internally, meaning that the sons and daughters of professionals are likely to end up as professionals themselves.
- The position of professional workers is based on the possession of educational qualifications and a long period of training, i.e. university followed by professional examinations.
- Savage argues that professionals have economic capital (i.e. a very good standard of living and savings) and cultural capital (they see the worth of education and other cultural assets such as taste in high culture) which they pass on to their children.
- Professionals have strong occupational associations that protect and actively pursue their interests (e.g. the Law Society, the British Medical Association) although lower down the professional ladder, these associations/unions become weaker (e.g. teachers' unions).
- Higher professionals enjoy high rewards, status and job security.
- Professionals are aware of their common interests and are willing to take collective action to protect those interests.
- Professionals have a greater sense of class identity than other middle-class groups.

Managers

- Savage suggests that managers have assets based upon a particular skill within specific organisations, and these are not easily transferable to other companies or industries.
- Many managers have been upwardly mobile from the routine white-collar sector, or the skilled working class, and consequently they lack qualifications such as degrees.
- Managerial social position is likely to be the result of experience and reputation rather than qualifications.
- Most managers do not belong to professional associations or trade unions. Consequently, they are more individualistic, less likely to identify a common collectivist interest with their fellow managers, and much more likely to see fellow managers as competitors.
- Savage argues that managers encourage their children to pursue higher education because they can see the benefits of a professional career.
- Managers, despite having economic capital (they are well paid), are less likely to have the cultural capital possessed by professionals.

- Savage argues that job security differentiates professionals from managers — managers are less likely to have this and are constantly under threat from recession, mergers, downsizing and so on.
- Savage points out that middle managers, such as bank managers, may find themselves unemployed, downwardly mobile into the routine white-collar sector or becoming self-employed rather than becoming higher managers such as company directors.

White-collar workers and proletarianisation

- Marxists, such as Harry Braverman, argue that routine white-collar workers are no longer middle class because they have been subjected to a process of **proletarianisation**, i.e. they have lost the social and economic advantages that they enjoyed over manual workers, such as superior pay and working conditions.
- Braverman argues that in the past 20 years employers have used technology, especially computers, to break down complex, white-collar skills, such as book-keeping, into simplistic routine tasks. This process is known as **deskilling** and is an attempt to increase output, maximise efficiency and reduce costs.
- These developments have been accompanied by the parallel development of **feminising** the routine white-collar workforce, especially in the financial sector — female workers are generally cheaper to employ and are seen by employers as more adaptable and amenable to this type of work.
- Braverman concludes that deskilling means that occupations that were once middle class are now indistinguishable from those of manual workers. Many routine white-collar workers, who are mainly women, now have similar conditions of work and pay to blue-collar workers.

Evaluation

- Research by Devine suggests that there are still distinct cultural differences in terms of values, lifestyles and political attitudes between manual workers and white-collar workers.
- White-collar workers still generally enjoy advantages at work such as flexitime, fringe benefits, longer holidays and safer working conditions compared with manual workers.
- The NS–SEC recognises that there may be some overlap between white-collar workers and skilled manual workers and therefore does not play up the traditional blue-collar and white-collar distinction in its categorisation of occupations.
- There is a lack of convincing empirical research in this field, especially of upper-class and professional/management occupational groups.

The working class

Until the late twentieth century the working class had a strong sense of its social class position. Lockwood's 1966 research found that many workers, especially in industrial areas, subscribed to a value system he called **proletarian traditionalist**. Workers felt a strong sense of loyalty to each other because of shared work experience.

Consequently, workers were mutually supportive and had a keen sense of class solidarity and consciousness. They therefore tended to see society in terms of conflict — 'them versus us'. Research since this period has suggested significant changes have taken place within the working class.

- It was argued in the 1960s by Zweig that a section of the working class, the skilled manual workers (the 'labour aristocracy'), had adopted the economic and cultural lifestyle of the middle class. This became known as the **embourgeoisement thesis**.
- However, Goldthorpe and Lockwood's Affluent Worker study in the late 1960s found little evidence to support Zweig's assertion, although they did spot signs of 'convergence' between working-class and middle-class lifestyles.
- Goldthorpe and Lockwood identified the emergence of an **instrumental collectivist** (sometimes called **privatised instrumentalist**) worker who saw work as a means to an end rather than as a source of class identity.
- These affluent workers were more home-centred, were less likely to join trade unions or vote Labour, and were found in the newer manufacturing industries mainly situated in the south.
- Instrumental collectivists took industrial action in pursuit of higher pay or to protect living standards relative to other groups of workers, who they perceived as better off, rather than because of a shared class identity.

Evaluation

- Marxists reject the view that there is a fragmented working class and argue that there is a unified working class made up of manual workers, both black and white, male and female, and routine white-collar workers.
- The fact that some groups do not see themselves subjectively as working class is dismissed by Marxists as false class consciousness.
- Marxists argue that in relation to the means and social relations of production, all so-called 'class fractions' are objectively working class because they are alienated and exploited by the ruling class, whether they realise it or not.

Key concepts

the upper class; the establishment; the unified property class; the super class; social closure; petit-bourgeoisie; professionals; economic capital; cultural capital; high culture; the middle classes; class fractions; white-collar workers; proletarianisation; deskilling; collectivistic action; false class consciousness; instrumental collectivism; proletarian traditionalist; embourgeoisement; convergence; labour aristocracy; class solidarity; class identity

The underclass

The underclass thesis separates the underclass from the working class. The New Right version of this theory blames the victim.

- The New Right argues that the underclass is a distinct social group that exists in the inner cities and on council estates, and subscribes to a 'way of life' or culture

made up of deviant values and norms such as being workshy and welfare dependent, lacking commitment to family life and engaging in criminality.
- The underclass is allegedly reproduced generation by generation as parents socialise their children into this culture.
- The welfare state is seen as perpetuating such a system because knowledge that benefits are available demotivates people in their search for work.

Evaluation
- The structural view of the underclass stresses that structural obstacles, beyond the control of individuals, are responsible for their poverty and encourage fatalism and dependency. Many people are long-term unemployed because of recession or the fact that goods can be produced more cheaply in less economically developed countries.
- Groups such as ethnic minorities may be denied access to jobs and decent housing because of racism.
- Single mothers may find it impossible to return to work because of a lack of free or affordable childcare.
- The underclass is scapegoated for its position at the bottom of the socio-economic hierarchy.

Is social class dead or declining in importance?

Since the 1990s, postmodernist sociologists have argued that class has ceased to be the prime determinant of identity. It has been suggested that societies today are organised around consumption rather than production. Consequently, people now identify themselves in terms of what they consume rather than in terms of social class.
- Postmodernists argue that class identity has fragmented into numerous separate and individualised identities. Pakulski and Waters (1996) argue that people exercise more choice about the type of people they want to be.
- Postmodernists argue that gender, ethnicity, age, region and family role all interact and combine with consumption and media images to construct postmodern culture and identity.

Evaluation
- Marshall's survey indicates that social class is still a significant source of identity for many, and that members of a range of classes are aware of class differences and are happy to identify themselves using class categories.
- Postmodernists conveniently ignore the fact that consumption depends on jobs and levels of income. Poverty can inhibit any desire to pursue a postmodern lifestyle.
- The evidence regarding class differences in areas such as education and health overwhelmingly indicates the continuing importance of social class.

Key concepts
underclass; welfare dependency; New Right; postmodernism; consumption; choice

Synoptic evidence of the continuing importance of social class

Evidence for the continuing importance of social class can be taken from across the specification. Note the word 'evidence'. Statistical trends and patterns and empirical studies count as evidence; pure theory does not. Below are some examples of the types of evidence that would support the continuing importance of social class, taken from the fields of health and education. Other areas of the specification, such as the family, media, crime and deviance, and social policy and welfare, can be just as fertile in providing such evidence, as you will see in the Question and Answer section.

Health evidence

If illness were a chance occurrence, we would expect to see it randomly distributed across the population. However, we can see that some groups can expect disproportionate amounts of illness.

- Working-class people experience poorer mortality and morbidity rates than the middle class. More than 3,500 more working-class babies would survive per year if the working-class infant mortality rate was reduced to middle-class levels.
- If we compare causes of death, we can see that between 1972 and 1993, death rates for professionals from all causes fell by 44%, while the rate fell by only 10% for the unskilled.
- Death rates due to lung cancer among professionals fell by 58%, but the unskilled rate fell by only 25%.
- Death rates due to coronary heart disease fell by 58% among professionals, but the unskilled rate fell by only 3%.
- Working-class people are more likely to die before retirement of cancer, stroke and heart disease than middle-class people.
- There are a number of empirical studies, e.g. Roberts, Wilkinson, Tudor Hart, which attempt through the use of social surveys and official statistics to construct explanations for the poor levels of working-class health, and superior middle-class health, on the basis of data or evidence.
- Studies of poverty also link poor health to various aspects of economic deprivation.

Education evidence

At all stages of education, students from working-class backgrounds achieve less than their middle-class counterparts. Even when working-class children have the same level of intelligence as middle-class children, they are:

- less likely to attend nursery schools or preschool play-groups
- more likely to start school unable to read
- more likely to fall behind in reading, writing and maths skills
- more likely to be placed in lower sets or streams
- more likely to get fewer GCSEs, or low grades
- more likely to leave school at the age of 16
- less likely to go into the sixth form and on to university

A number of empirical studies, e.g. Douglas, Halsey, Wedge and Prosser, Ball, Willis, attempt through the use of social surveys, official statistics and observation to construct explanations for class differences in education.

Studies of poverty (see below) also link educational underachievement to various aspects of economic deprivation.

Poverty as a dimension of inequality

Concepts and measures of poverty

There are four main sociological ways of looking at poverty, in terms of definition and measurement.

(1) Absolute or subsistence models and measurements of poverty

Measures of absolute poverty are based on the idea that minimum resources can be identified as necessary to maintain human life, i.e. survival.
- Such measurements involve a judgement about basic human needs.
- Resources are identified, such as diet/nutritional intake, clothing, shelter and heating, that are required to maintain health and physical efficiency.
- Absolute definitions often involve defining an absolute poverty line in terms of income, and describing all those who fall beneath such a line as experiencing poverty.
- Governments tend to use official poverty lines based on income to determine who is eligible for state benefits, such as income support and housing benefits.
- Broader definitions of absolute poverty go beyond basic needs to include cultural needs, such as access to education and health care.

Evaluation
- Basic needs are not universal — rather they are relative to particular societies and social groups. Basic nutritional needs in Ethiopia are different to those in the UK. ·
- Even within the UK it is likely that needs differ according to social group, region etc. For example, the basic nutritional needs of the elderly are different from those of pregnant women or new mothers.
- In some societies, especially Western societies, amenities and goods previously described as 'comforts' and 'luxuries' have become necessities, e.g. household goods such as flush toilets, fridges and carpets.

- Social expectations of needs, comforts and luxuries constantly change.
- Definitions of basic needs in sociological explanations of poverty often reflect Western views.

(2) The budget standards approach

The budget standards approach is a variation on the absolute poverty model and involves calculating the value or budget of a set of consumer items, such as the food needed for an individual or a family.

Rowntree's studies of poverty in York (1899, 1931 and 1951) are good examples of this approach.

- Rowntree's 1899 study estimated that 33% of the people of York were in poverty because they fell below a poverty line based on a minimum weekly sum of money needed to obtain the necessities of a healthy life. This was worked out by Rowntree after consulting with experts.
- Using this approach in 1931 and 1951, Rowntree concluded that poverty had largely been eradicated by the early 1950s.
- Research in the 1980s and 1990s by Bradshaw et al. used a variation on this approach — the study estimated how families spent their money, rather than relying on how experts felt they should spend it.
- Bradshaw et al. found that income support levels sustained very low standards of living. Families could not afford holidays and their diets did not contain sufficient calories for good health.

Evaluation
- The budget standards approach may be over-dependent upon value judgements from experts about what constitutes an adequate income or standard of living.
- Whether you agree that somebody is in poverty may depend upon your political stance.
- People's quality of life is not always shaped by how they spend money — it can be enhanced, for example, by support from extended family.

Key concepts
absolute poverty; subsistence poverty; poverty line; basic needs; cultural needs

(3) Relative poverty models and measurement

Some researchers insist that in a constantly changing world, no definition of needs can be absolute. Standards of living frequently change as social expectations change. Sociologists who use relative definitions and measurements of poverty insist that people are poor if they are involuntarily excluded from the cultural lifestyle that the majority of the population takes for granted.

Townsend's surveys
- Townsend notes that poverty as a condition derives from the cultural norms and social expectations of particular societies. What we eat and drink, for example, is

largely determined by the lifestyle of the culture to which we belong.

- Relative poverty or deprivation is the denial of access to those resources and lifestyles taken for granted by the communities in which we live.
- Poverty is the inability to participate in normal and socially approved activities, ordinary living patterns, customs etc.
- In 1968, Townsend operationalised relative poverty by constructing a 'deprivation index' of 60 resources and activities taken for granted by 2,052 households, according to a questionnaire survey.
- He selected 12 items as universal symbols of deprivation and concluded that households bringing in an income of less than 150% of the level of supplementary benefit (equivalent to today's income support) were more likely to be deprived of these items.
- On this basis, he calculated that 22.9% of the population of the UK were in poverty in 1968–69.
- In later research, carried out in London in 1985–86, Townsend modified his operationalisation of relative poverty. Based on a sample of 2,703 people, he distinguished between 'material deprivation' (diet, clothing, housing etc.) and 'social deprivation' (lack of employment rights, educational deprivation, poor health etc.) and compiled a deprivation index of 70 items.
- He also distinguished between 'objective deprivation' (measured by the deprivation index) and 'subjective deprivation' (the income people thought they needed to escape poverty).

Evaluation

- Some sociologists have criticised the content of the indexes as arbitrary and based on Townsend's subjective judgements, i.e. for not being objective enough.
- Relative definitions of poverty are eternal, i.e. such poverty will only be eradicated if everybody shares the same experiences.
- Townsend had no means of telling whether the deprivation was a result of a shortage of money, inappropriate spending or choice.
+ In Townsend's defence, his poverty indexes are underpinned by mass surveys, i.e. he went to some lengths to check whether what he saw as being symbols of relative poverty were shared by representative samples of the population.

The Breadline Britain surveys

- The Breadline Britain surveys of relative poverty conducted by Mack and Lansley in 1983 and 1990 distinguished between styles of living which people could not afford, and those they chose not to adopt.
- The 1983 study operationalised poverty in three stages. First, by asking 1,174 people what they considered to be necessities, Mack and Lansley looked for a majority consensus on what were socially approved essential items and activities. Second, they asked the sample population what they lacked from this consensual index. People were considered poor if they lacked three or more items/activities on the list. Third, they asked the sample population whether their 'deprivation' was a matter of choice or not.

- Using this method, Mack and Lansley calculated that 7.5 million people or 13.8% of the population were in poverty.
- In a follow-up study in 1990 using a sample of 1,800 people, they noted that consensus about what counted as necessities had changed, and adjusted the index accordingly to calculate that 11 million people were living in poverty.
- Two thirds of the poor identified by Mack and Lansley were dependent upon state benefits, especially the elderly (who made up one fifth of the poor) and single parents (two thirds of these were poor).

Evaluation

- Comparability between the 1983 and 1990 surveys is a problem because of changes in the number of necessities.
- The opinion surveys still depend upon the subjective judgement of Mack and Lansley, who chose the initial lists of potential necessities.
- The decision to define poverty as lacking three or more items seems arbitrary — why not four or five?
- Perhaps people cannot afford necessities because they are spending money on non-necessities, such as cigarettes and alcohol.
- Mack and Lansley's definition of 'necessities' needs to be more specific. 'Three meals a day for children' could include a nutritionally balanced meal or a Big Mac with French fries.
- The sample population was not given the opportunity to contribute ideas or experiences to the operationalisation of necessities.
+ Relative definitions such as those used by Mack and Lansley are really a combination of relative judgements (about what is taken for granted as 'normal' in a particular culture or time period) and absolute judgements (a minimum number of necessities is calculated as essential to lift people out of poverty).

Key concepts

relative poverty; cultural norms; deprivation index; operationalisation; material deprivation; social deprivation; objective deprivation; subjective deprivation; consensual index

(4) The social exclusion model

Some sociologists prefer the term 'social exclusion' to 'poverty'. This term refers to being excluded from access not only to material resources, but also to social, economic, political and cultural resources.

- The Left Realists, Young and Lea, note that young black males in inner city areas experience social exclusion because:
  - they are economically deprived due to high levels of unemployment because of factors such as employer racism
  - they are politically excluded or marginalised, because they lack the power to influence mainstream political parties
  - they do not enjoy the same educational opportunities as their white peers, due to possible institutional racism in the state education system

- The concept of exclusion implies that sociologists should look at the power of the excluders. For example, why are young blacks marginalised by white society?
- The model also implies that social change to eradicate poverty must be holistic, i.e. social policy must aim to give people the chance to participate fully in all areas of social life.
- New Labour has set itself the task of making sure that all groups, and specifically single parents and the unemployed, feel a sense of 'social inclusion', i.e. feel they can participate in all areas of social life.

Evaluation

- Social exclusion/inclusion are difficult to define or operationalise, and are consequently hard to measure precisely.
- Social exclusion/inclusion are relative in that different societies, and ideological or political groups within the same societies, may define them in different ways.
- It may be impossible to tackle some aspects of social exclusion, such as the negative stereotyping of powerless groups through media moral panics, or the decline in community.
- Poverty may be a more useful concept than social exclusion because it is a more emotional term that inspires and motivates people to do something about it.
+ The concept of social exclusion draws our attention to the fact that poverty takes many diverse forms and has different degrees of influence over an individual's life.

Key concepts

left realism; social exclusion; marginalisation; social inclusion

Other means of measuring poverty

- Examination of income distribution by Goodman and Webb shows that between 1979 and 1992, the poorest 10% of the population's income fell by 18%, while the richest 10% of the population's income rose by 61%. In other words, the poorest 10% got even poorer.
- In 1995, there were 125,000 people registered as homeless by local authorities, 22,000 living in bed and breakfast accommodation, and a significant 'dark figure' of mainly young, homeless people living on the streets who are not officially registered with local authorities.

Contemporary trends in poverty

Note the synoptic evidence that can be gathered from the facts below.

Women and poverty

Some sociologists claim there has been a 'feminisation of poverty', for several reasons.

- Poverty is common among the elderly, and female pensioners tend to outlive male pensioners.

- 90% of lone parents are female.
- Women generally do not earn as much as men.
- Women are less likely to have occupational pensions because they may have spent substantial periods of their lives in the home as mothers and housewives.
- Women are more likely to be in low-status, low-skilled and therefore low-paid jobs even in the service sector.
- More women than men work part-time.
- More women are excluded from work because they are full-time carers.
- Women may be excluded from sections of the job market because of employer stereotyping and discrimination — such employers are likely to see women's primary role as domestic and/or maternal.
- Women may be denied access to professional and managerial jobs because of institutionalised discrimination in the form of the 'glass ceiling'.
- Women may experience poverty in the form of ill health. Evidence from Bernard and Graham suggests that married and especially housebound mothers are more likely to suffer ill health (particularly poor mental health) than men.
- Women are often excluded from claiming state benefits such as pensions, tax allowances and so on by a patriarchal welfare state.
- Women experience what Lister calls 'time poverty'. Young mothers do not enjoy the same leisure time as fathers, because they tend to take ultimate responsibility for childcare and domestic chores.
- Poverty may be responsible for specific types of female crime, such as prostitution, shoplifting and welfare fraud.

Ethnicity and poverty

- All ethnic minority groups are more likely to experience poverty than white people.
- There is variation in the experience of poverty across ethnic minority groups; Bangladeshi and Pakistani households are most at risk.
- One of the main causes of poverty among these groups is exclusion from the labour market — there is evidence that racism by employers may play some role here.
- Another main cause of poverty among ethnic minorities is exploitation of their labour in the form of low pay.
- Alcock identifies a range of different forms of poverty and exclusion that ethnic minorities in the UK experience, including lack of access to good quality private housing, poor access to aspects of the welfare state such as health and welfare benefits, educational inequalities, lack of political representation, being the victims of negative media stereotyping and over-zealous policing, and physical harm and fear from racist attacks.
- Institutional racism across a range of organisations is increasingly recognised as a cause of poverty.
- Many of these aspects of exclusion reinforce each other. Poor, damp housing can lead to poor health in children, time off school and, in the long term, few qualifications. This in turn leads to low-skilled and low-paid jobs or unemployment.

Social class and poverty

Regardless of whether the poor are mainly female or members of particular ethnic minority groups, Kempson found that the experience of poverty brings about various socioeconomic disadvantages, including:

- debt
- high levels of marital breakdown, especially divorce
- poor diet and nutritional intake, which results in poor immune systems and consequently higher levels of morbidity
- allocation of children to failing schools in inner city areas
- high levels of educational failure, truancy and exclusion
- allocation to housing estates characterised by crime, drug abuse and unsuitable, deteriorating housing stock
- disproportionate attention from the police, social workers etc.
- newspaper reporting which stereotypes the poor as undeserving and idle welfare scroungers

Treasury figures from March 1999 estimate that up to 25% of children never escape from poverty and that economic deprivation is passed down the generations by underachievement in schools and unemployment.

Key concepts

feminisation of poverty; time poverty; patriarchal welfare state; institutional racism

The underclass debate: theories of culture and poverty

There are three interrelated theories of poverty which tend to blame the victim, i.e. claim that the responsibility for being in poverty lies with the individual or the cultural weaknesses of a socially deprived group.

(1) The culture of dependency thesis

- Marsland argues that poverty has become confused with inequality — the latter concept is a good thing, because it motivates people to compete and work harder.
- He says that real poverty has largely been eradicated by capitalism.
- He argues that poverty statistics are artificially created because they are largely determined by the number of people claiming welfare benefits.
- According to Marsland, universal welfare benefits are too generous and have led to the emergence of a culture of dependency, in which inadequate people are encouraged to abandon self-reliance and responsibility for their own welfare.

Evaluation

- Marsland uses evidence selectively and ignores recent evidence showing that the income of the poorest 10% has fallen since 1979.

content guidance

- He neglects those groups in poverty who are not dependent on the welfare state for benefits, e.g. the low paid and women.
- Jordan claims that Marsland has exaggerated the impact of universal benefits as the system is mean in its treatment of deprived groups — a truly universal system, he argues, would free people from dependence.
- Research by Dear and Taylor-Gooby indicates that long-term claimants want to work and there is no evidence of a dependency culture.

Key concepts

victim-blaming; culture of dependency; selective/universal benefits

(2) The culture of poverty thesis

- It is claimed by New Right sociologists that the poor differ from members of mainstream society in terms of their social characteristics and lifestyles.
- Their norms and values supposedly have produced a 'design for living' which is transmitted from one generation to the next.
- This culture of poverty is supposedly characterised by strong feelings of marginalisation (i.e. lack of power), dependence on others (especially the state), inadequacy and fatalism (resigned acceptance and therefore inability to act for change).

Evaluation

- There is little empirical evidence supporting the notion of a unified culture of poverty with values and norms distinct from those of mainstream society.
- The lifestyle of the poor varies, while research suggests that their outlooks are similar to those held by mainstream society.
- Many sociologists see the behaviour of the poor as a realistic response to 'situational constraints'. This means that their behaviour is shaped by social influences, over which they have no control, e.g. unemployment due to economic recession, low pay, globalisation, the restructuring of work and mechanisation.

Key concepts

culture of poverty; design for living; marginalisation; fatalism; situational constraints

(3) The underclass thesis

- Charles Murray (1989) argues that an underclass or 'new rabble' has emerged in Britain: a minority of poor people, characterised not by poverty but by 'deplorable behaviour' and lifestyles which revolve around voluntary long-term unemployment, crime, immoral sexual behaviour etc.
- Among the underclass, Murray argues, illegitimacy and absent fathers are the norm and this results in inadequate socialisation as children grow up. Consequently, there is a high potential for future delinquency, crime and immorality.
- Murray considers that rising crime rates are linked to an emerging underclass.
- He argues that unemployment is largely the result of young men electing not to work because they fail to see work as a source of status and self-respect.

- Like Marsland, Murray feels that these attitudes are exacerbated by an over-generous welfare state which encourages a culture of dependency among the underclass.

Evaluation

- There is little empirical evidence for the existence of an underclass — Murray's evidence is largely assertion and anecdote rather than hard scientific fact.
- Brown and Madge's research on those born into disadvantaged homes found that most did not end up disadvantaged themselves.
- Murray neglects situational constraints deriving from international recession, government policy etc.
- Heath's research into people who claimed income support found that most wanted a paid job, that they valued marriage and had 'normal' ambitions.
- Murray makes sweeping generalisations about lone parenthood.
- Field agrees that an underclass has emerged but does not see this as having a distinctive culture — rather what unites this underclass is a common negative experience of social change and the government policies that have led to high levels of unemployment, poverty etc.
- Field also notes the emergence of a more individualistic and selfish society that is happy to scapegoat, especially via media moral panics, those who are less economically successful.
- Craine's 1997 research in an inner city area of Manchester found little evidence that youths were workshy.
- Craine found that both teenage motherhood and street crime were often the only realistic alternative, given the low level of welfare benefits.

Key concepts

underclass; new rabble; inadequate socialisation

Explanations of inequality and difference

Class-based theories of stratification and inequality

Functionalism

Functionalists argue that stratification and inequality perform a positive function for society. For example, Davis and Moore say that stratification makes a contribution to social order — therefore, class inequality is beneficial, positive and necessary. The functionalist theory of class stresses the following:

- All societies have to ensure that their most functionally important and senior positions are filled by people who are talented and efficient.
- Talent and skill, however, are in short supply and top jobs require an intensive amount of training and time to acquire the necessary expertise.
- Class societies are essentially meritocracies — high rewards in the form of income and status are guaranteed in order to motivate gifted people to make the necessary sacrifices in terms of education and training.
- Members of society generally agree that stratification is necessary because education socialises them into accepting meritocratic principles, which involves the acceptance of unequal patterns of rewards. There is 'value consensus'.
- Qualifications and therefore the stratification system function to allocate all individuals to an occupational role that suits their abilities (role allocation).
- Class position is therefore a fair reflection of people's talents.
- Stratification encourages all members of society to work to the best of their ability. For example, those at the top will wish to retain their advantages, while those placed below will wish to improve on their position.

Evaluation

- There is little consensus about rewards. There appears to be a substantial level of resentment about the unequal distribution of income and wealth as illustrated by the controversy over 'fat-cat' levels of pay.
- Davis and Moore suggest that unequal rewards are the product of consensus, but they may be the result of some groups being able to use economic and political power to increase their rewards against the will of others.
- High rewards also go to people who play no functionally important role but simply live off the interest on their wealth.
- Many occupations can be seen to be functionally essential to the smooth running of society but are not highly rewarded, e.g. nursing.
- Davis and Moore neglect the dysfunctions of stratification, e.g. that poverty is a major problem for people and negatively impacts on mortality, health, education and family life.

Key concepts

functional; meritocracy; value consensus; role allocation; dysfunction

Marxism

Marxists see all history as the history of class struggle. Apart from a primitive form of communism which existed in early hunting and gathering societies, all stages of history, such as ancient slavery, feudalism and capitalism, have been characterised by class-based societies. The Marxist theory of class stresses the following:
- Social class is essentially the product of the mode of production of a society.
- The mode of production of capitalist societies is industrial, whereas in feudal societies it was agricultural.
- The mode of production is made up of the relationship between the means of production and the social relations of production.

- The means of production refers to resources such as land, factories, machinery and raw materials, which are owned by the capitalist class or bourgeoisie.
- The workers or proletariat do not own productive property and their only asset is their labour power.
- The social relations of production refers to the economic relationship between the bourgeoisie and proletariat, as the latter hires out its labour power to the former.
- The relationship between the bourgeoisie and proletariat is deeply unequal, exploitative and creates class conflict.
- Inequality, exploitation and conflict result from the fact that it is in the interests of the capitalist class to keep wages low in order to increase profits.
- The bourgeoisie therefore seizes the surplus value of working-class labour.
- Capitalism's relentless pursuit of profit means that workers lose control over the work process as new technology is introduced, thus creating the potential for alienation.
- However, workers rarely think that they are being exploited because they are suffering from false class consciousness — they have been fooled by ideological apparatuses such as education and the media into believing that capitalism is fair and natural.

Evaluation

- Marxism is an economic determinist or reductionist theory in that all major ideas are seen to be the product of the economic relationship between the bourgeoisie and proletariat. However, conflicts around nationalism, ethnicity and gender cannot be explained adequately in economic terms.
- Marx made certain predictions, for example that the working class would experience poverty and misery, the middle class would disappear, and that communism would replace capitalism, which have not come true.
- The living standards of the working class have risen, the middle class has grown and communism was eventually rejected in Eastern Europe.
- Western class-based capitalist societies may have problems such as poverty and homelessness, but they have a good record in terms of democracy and trade union rights.
- The working class may be sensibly reconciled to capitalism, rather than falsely conscious.

Key concepts

class struggle; mode of production; means of production; social relations of production; bourgeoisie; proletariat; labour power; exploitation; class conflict; surplus value; alienation; false class consciousness; ideological apparatus

Max Weber

Weber was critical of Marx for neglecting the sources of power that did not arise primarily out of economic relationships. The Weberian theory of class includes the following points:

- Weber saw class and status as two separate but related sources of power, which have separate but related effects on people's life chances (their chances of getting on well in terms of jobs, health etc.).
- Weber defined class in terms of market position, e.g. income, skills and qualifications, rather than purely ownership of productive property. He consequently recognised that within the working class, there are a range of life chances.
- Status inequality can derive from class inequality. People who occupy high occupational roles generally have high social status, but this can also derive from other sources of power such as gender, race, religion etc.
- Weber noted that status was also linked to consumption styles (i.e. how people spend their money). Some people derive status from conspicuous consumption, such as being seen to buy expensive designer products.
- This point has led to the postmodernist idea that in the twenty-first century, consumption style rather than social class structures people's identity. People no longer primarily think 'I am working class or middle class' but instead see themselves as consumers of various 'in' brands.

Evaluation

- Marxists argue that Weber was too wrapped up in identifying trivial market details, and neglected the basic split between capitalists and workers.
- Marxists argue that class and status are strongly linked — the capitalist class not only has wealth but also high status and political power. Weber recognised that these overlap but suggested that a person can have wealth but little status, e.g. a lottery winner.
- Marxists argue that gender and ethnic differences are essentially rooted in class differences, but Weber saw them as being separate and distinct.

Key concepts

status; consumption; conspicuous consumption; market position

Gender-based theories of stratification and inequality

Dual labour market theory

The 'dual labour market' theory of Barron and Norris focuses on gender inequalities in employment. They argue that there exist two markets for labour — the primary sector characterised by secure, well-paid jobs with long-term promotion prospects, dominated by men, and the secondary sector, characterised by insecure, low-paid, unskilled jobs. Barron and Norris point out that women are more likely to be found in the secondary sector. They are less likely to gain primary-sector employment because:

- employers subscribe to stereotypical beliefs about the unsuitability of women, e.g. employers may believe that women's careers are likely to be interrupted by producing and rearing children, and may not invest in training for them

- promotion streams are organised in ways which match the life experiences of men better than women, because employers demand continuous service
- as Caplow argues, the husband's career and the cultural pressure on women to have children may dictate the geographical movement of the family, and consequently undermine the continuity in women's careers
- the legal and political framework supporting women is weak, e.g. both the Equal Pay Act and Sex Discrimination Act are feeble laws which fail to protect women's employment rights
- this theory stresses that the social organisation of work in Western societies is essentially patriarchal, which makes discrimination against women 'natural' and possible

This theory undermines the popular assumption that better qualifications and increased ambition for women would automatically dismantle gender divisions in employment. Women with the same qualifications will continue to be disadvantaged as long as these two sectors exist and are underpinned by patriarchal assumptions about the role of women.

Evaluation
- Bradley points out that the theory fails to explain inequalities within the same sector. For example, teaching is not a secondary labour market, yet women are less likely than men to gain high status jobs in this profession.

Key concepts
dual labour market; primary/secondary sectors; patriarchy

Liberal feminism

Liberal feminists argue that gender roles are largely socially constructed through the socialisation process, primarily in the family, but also through such secondary agencies as the education system and the mass media. In other words, gender role socialisation is responsible for reproducing a sexual division of labour in which masculinity is largely seen as dominant and femininity as subordinate.
- Liberal feminist research in the 1970s, in particular, focused on how the dominant images of females, disseminated by such agencies as school and mass media, stressed marriage as a priority, and education and careers as being secondary.
- In the 1990s, liberal feminists suggested that these processes were coming to an end. Both Sue Lees' and Sue Sharpe's work on the attitudes of teenage girls suggest that education and careers are now a priority for young women, while females have also enjoyed great educational success in recent years.
- Ann Oakley argues that the main reason for the subordination of women in the labour market is the dominance of the mother–housewife role for women.
- Oakley argues that ideas such as the maternal instinct and maternal deprivation serve primarily to ensure men's dominance of the labour market. Oakley found that part-time women workers gave responsibility to their husband and children as their main reason for not taking up full-time work.

- Sylvia Walby (1990) suggests that although there is evidence that masculinity and femininity are socially constructed, it does not explain why this leads to men dominating and women being oppressed.
- Liberal feminism implies that people passively accept their gender identities — it underestimates the degree of resistance by women.
- Liberal feminism does not explain why masculine and feminine identities are the way they are.
- Liberal feminism fails to acknowledge that women's experiences differ according to social class and race.
- Some liberal feminists advise caution in our interpretation of educational and occupational trends. Women are still located in educational and job ghettoes, especially in higher education, and many commentators have observed that representations of women in the mass media are still very sexist.

Key concepts

liberal feminism; gender role socialisation; sexual division of labour; subordination; resistance

Marxist feminism

Marxist feminists suggest that women form a classic example of a 'reserve army of labour'. This comprises a body of people who are drawn upon by prosperous firms in times of rapid expansion and disposed of when recession sets in. Women constitute a more disposable part of the workforce for a number of reasons:

- Women change jobs more frequently than men so they are more vulnerable at times of redundancy.
- Women are generally less skilled, relatively under-unionised and often part-time. Consequently, it is easier for employers to sack them.
- Capitalist ideologies locate women in the home. The ideology that married women have less right to a job than men is common among management, unions and women themselves. When women are made unemployed, such ideology suggests that 'women have gone back to their proper jobs'.

Evaluation

- The reserve army of labour theory has been criticised because it does not explain why male and female labour is put to different uses — it fails to explain why there are men's jobs and women's jobs.
- The theory fails to explain why women occupy the housewife role.
- Moreover, if women are cheaper than men, surely capitalists would get rid of the more expensive men first, i.e. men's jobs would be more insecure.

Key concepts

reserve army of labour; capitalism; ideology

Triple-systems theory

Sylvia Walby's 'triple systems theory' develops the concept of patriarchy to explain gender stratification. She suggests that patriarchy has three elements to it:

(1) **Subordination** — patriarchal institutions like the family, media and education inevitably produce unequal relations between men and women.

(2) **Oppression** — women experience sexism because men discriminate against them on the basis of unfounded stereotypes or ideology.

(3) **Exploitation** — men exploit women's skills and labour without rewarding them sufficiently, e.g. in the home.

Walby argues that patriarchy is not only about the interaction of men and women in these three respects, but that it also intersects with capitalism and racism to produce gender stratification. Such inequality can be seen in six social structures:

(1) The patriarchal mode of production, which exploits female labour within the family.

(2) The fact of patriarchal relations in paid work, as reflected in vertical and horizontal segregation at work.

(3) Patriarchal relations in the state — the state acts in the interests of men rather than women, e.g. in terms of taxation, welfare rules and the weakness of laws protecting women at work.

(4) Acts of male violence against women, such as rape and domestic violence, persist as major social problems.

(5) A sexual double standard exists, which endorses multiple sexual partners for men but condemns the same behaviour in women.

(6) Agencies like the mass media represent women in narrow social roles, e.g. as sex objects and mother–housewives.

Catherine Hakim and rational choice theory

Catherine Hakim is extremely critical of all the previous feminist positions. She argues that feminist theories of patriarchy are both inaccurate and misleading, and that women are not victims of unfair employment practices. According to Hakim:

- Women with children make rational choices about their futures — they believe that childcare is as important a career as employment.
- The lack of women in top jobs and their domination of part-time work does not reflect lack of free childcare, employer discrimination or weak laws but reflects the rational choice to put children and family first.

Evaluation

- Ginn and Arber point out that all too often it is employer attitudes rather than women's attitudes that confine women to the secondary labour market.

Key concepts

rational choice; subordination; oppression; discrimination; exploitation; patriarchy

Definitions of race and ethnicity

- Racism refers to a combination of discriminatory practices, unequal relations and power, and negative beliefs and attitudes.
- Prejudice means a style of thinking which relies heavily on stereotypes. These are usually factually incorrect, exaggerated and distorted.
- Discrimination is defined as prejudice put into practice in regard to jobs, housing, racial attacks and perhaps even policing.
- Institutional racism is the idea that racist assumptions are built into the rules and routines of Britain's social institutions, so that the specific needs of ethnic minorities are neglected. This type of racism is taken for granted and habitual — in other words, it has become so institutionalised that it is not recognised as racism. Both the Home Office and the London Metropolitan Police have recently admitted that their organisations are institutionally racist.

Theories of ethnic inequalities

Weberian explanations

- Parkin argues that modern societies are characterised by class inequality and ethnic inequality, but status and power are in the hands of the majority ethnic group. This makes it difficult for ethnic minority groups to compete equally for jobs, housing etc.
- Ethnic minority members who do manual jobs are technically part of the working class, but are likely to face prejudice and discrimination from the white working class because they suffer from status inequality in addition to class inequality.
- Even middle-class Asians doing professional jobs may experience status inequality in the form of prejudicial attitudes held by members of both the white middle and working classes.
- The Weberian dual labour market theory of Barron and Norris argues that there are two markets for labour — the primary sector, characterised by secure, well-paid jobs with long-term promotion prospects (dominated by white men), and the secondary sector, characterised by low-paid, unskilled and insecure jobs (dominated by women and black people).
- Ethnic minorities are less likely to gain primary-sector employment because employers may subscribe to racist beliefs about their unsuitability, and even practise discrimination against them either when they apply for jobs or by denying them responsibility and promotion.
- The legal and political framework supporting black people is weak. The Race Relations Act, which is supposed to protect them from discriminatory practices, is generally thought to be feeble. Trade unions are generally white-dominated and tend to favour white workers.
- Some Weberians, especially Rex and Tomlinson, argue that ethnic minority experience of both class and status inequality, especially racism, can lead to poverty which is made more severe by racism. A black underclass may exist which is

marginalised, alienated and frustrated, and which sometimes erupts in the form of inner-city riots if young blacks feel, for example, that they are being harassed by the police.

Evaluation

– Commentators such as Murray and Marsland blame the culture of some ethnic minorities for their poverty and unemployment, in that they claim that young African-Caribbeans, in particular, are workshy and welfare-dependent. This is despite the fact that surveys indicate their norms and values with regard to work are no different from mainstream society.
– The existence of a black underclass has not been proved — there is considerable overlap between the white and black population in terms of poverty and unemployment.
+ However, the concept of status inequality may help to explain some apparent divisions between the white and black working class, in terms of unemployment and promotion into white-collar work.

Key concepts

racism; discrimination; prejudice; institutional racism; dual labour market; status inequality

Marxist explanations

Marxists are adamant that black people are part of the exploited working class and they generally see status inequality as less important than class inequality. However, they do acknowledge that racism is a powerful influence in modern society and suggest that it is generally used as an ideological weapon in order to attain three objectives:

(1) Racism means that black unemployment, low pay and poor conditions in the workplace do not generate controversy, thus ensuring that employers can treat black people as a reserve army of labour, to be hired when the economy expands and laid off when recession sets in.

(2) Marxists argue that white workers are encouraged to perceive black workers as a threat to their jobs, so that employers can use the threat of cheaper black workers to control their workforce — especially if there are hints that white workers are planning to strike for higher pay. This tactic 'divides and rules' the black and white working class, as white workers are encouraged to see black workers as a greater threat to their position than the organisation of capitalism.

(3) Social problems caused by the mismanagement of capitalism can also be blamed on visible ethnic minorities. Black people can be scapegoated for unemployment (through beliefs such as 'they've come over here to take our jobs') or inner-city decline ('this was a nice neighbourhood before they moved in').

Evaluation

– It is difficult to prove that racism is a capitalist ideology — it may benefit capitalism in the long term but this is not evidence that it functions exclusively as an ideological apparatus.

- Marxists tend to talk about racism as if the capitalist class had deliberately constructed it to control both black and white workers. However, although racism probably does benefit capitalism in the way Marxists argue, there is no evidence that the capitalist class is responsible for its existence or its maintenance.
- Miles argues that we should see ethnic minorities as members of 'racialised class fractions', meaning that although ethnic minorities are part of the working class, there are significant cultural differences between them and the white working class which result in them stressing aspects of their ethnic identity. Young African-Caribbeans, for example, may stress black power through membership of the Rastafarian sect or by stressing elements of black history, whilst Asians may stress family ties and community.
- Miles also notes that some ethnic minorities who are members of the middle class may see their interests lying with capitalism. The Asian emphasis on entre-preneurship, enterprise and mutual support may be advantageous in achieving business success.
- Miles points out that ethnicity probably means that the white middle class will never accept that Asian professionals have the same status as they have, and consequently may be unhappy at the idea of successful Asians moving into their neighbourhood, believing that it may bring down house prices.
- There is evidence that increasing numbers of ethnic minorities are entering the ranks of the professional middle class, although there is some evidence that they often end up in the lower-middle class, where status and pay are not high, or in lower and middle management rather than top management positions.

Key concepts

class inequality; reserve army of labour; divide and rule; racism as ideology; moral panic; scapegoating; racialised class fractions

Questions
&
Answers

This section of the guide provides you with five questions on the topic of **Social Inequality and Difference** in the style of the OCR examination. The first two questions are followed by a grade-C candidate response. These are on the right track but fail, for various reasons, to score very high marks.

Questions 1–4 all have a grade-A candidate response. It is important to note that these are not 'model' answers. These responses are not the only possible answers to these questions, nor are they necessarily the best. They represent one particular successful style; one that answers the question and demonstrates the appropriate skills, especially using suitable concepts and studies, displaying a critical and evaluative awareness towards the material used, and presenting a logically structured argument.

Don't make the mistake of learning the A-grade responses parrot-fashion. Remember that you have to be flexible and you have to be able to respond to the specific demands of a question. It would be quite possible, particularly in the answers to (c) and (d), to take a different approach, or to use different material, or even to come to a different conclusion, and still gain very high marks.

A fifth question is provided which is not accompanied by a student answer. It is followed by a plan of action, and you should use this to write your own response. It is recommended that you spend some time revising the topic before tackling this question. You should answer the question under timed conditions with no notes.

Examiner's comments

The candidate answers are accompanied by examiner's comments. These are preceded by the icon *e* and indicate where credit is due. For the grade-A answers, the examiner shows you what it is that enables the candidate to score so highly. Particular attention is given to the candidate's use of the examinable skills: knowledge and understanding; interpretation and analysis; and evaluation. For the grade-C answers, the examiner points out areas for improvement, specific problems and common errors. You are also invited to rewrite the answer in order to gain higher marks, and some pointers are given to show you how you might do this.

Poverty

Item A

Two million children in Britain — more than one in six — are experiencing multiple deprivation and poverty according to a major survey of poverty and social exclusion carried out by the Joseph Rowntree Foundation. The survey showed that between 1983 and 1999 the number of households living in poverty grew from 14% to 24%. Interviews with a nationally-representative sample of adults were used to draw up a checklist of household items and activities that a majority of people consider to be necessities that everyone should be able to afford and which they should not go without. A second survey was then conducted to discover how many individuals lacked these 'necessities of life' and gather other information on income and social exclusion. The study found that more than 2 million children are going without two or more necessities such as adequate clothing and a healthy diet. Around 9.5 million people cannot afford to keep their homes adequately heated.

Item B

The 'poverty trap' explanation of deprivation suggests that once people get into a situation of poverty it can be very difficult to get out. Paradoxically, it is expensive to be poor and those in poverty have to spend a lot just to maintain their current standard of living. For example, the poor cannot afford to insulate their homes and so pay higher fuel bills. They cannot afford to travel to cheap supermarkets out of town and so have to buy goods at the expensive cornershop. In addition, the welfare system is such that if someone in poverty gets an increase in income (say by getting a better paid job) the benefits they are entitled to are reduced so they end up no better off. Moreover, they are often trapped in deprived areas with poor schools. Consequently, their children may leave school with few qualifications and end up trapped in the same cycle of poverty.

Adapted from Trowler, P. (1996) *Investigating Health, Welfare and Poverty*, Collins.

(a) **Using only the information in Item A, identify two features of poverty in the UK today.** (6 marks)

(b) **Identify two reasons why 'it is expensive to be poor' according to Item B.** (6 marks)

(c) **Identify and explain two problems facing sociologists who use relative measurements of poverty.** (12 marks)

(d) **Using your wider sociological knowledge, outline the evidence for the view that poverty undermines the general life-chances of some social groups.** (22 marks)

(e) **Outline and assess sociological explanations for the persistence of poverty in the UK.** (44 marks)

Total: 90 marks

Answer to question 1: grade-C candidate

(a) Firstly, there are lots of children experiencing poverty in the UK today, and secondly, people lack the 'necessities of life'. This is because they are part of an underclass which does not care to work.

> *e* The candidate successfully identifies one feature of poverty according to Item A, i.e. relating to children, but the response is far too brief and does not make the most of the detail in the item in regard to this point. The second point made tells us little about poverty. Note that this candidate makes the mistake of offering an explanation that is not required and consequently wastes valuable time. The candidate would therefore only score 2 out of a possible 6 marks.

(b) Item B says it is expensive to be poor because the children of the poor leave school with no qualifications and end up in dead-end jobs with only low wages. It also says that the poor cannot afford to travel to out-of-town supermarkets and buy cheap food.

> *e* The first point is a valid one but it needed to be tied more closely to the idea that it is expensive to be poor. The second statement almost misses the point but does enough to earn 2 marks. The candidate would therefore be awarded 3 out of a possible 6 marks.

(c) Relative poverty is very difficult to measure. Not all sociologists agree with its use. Some sociologists prefer to use absolute definitions of poverty because a fixed sum of money can be worked out, e.g. to meet nutritional needs, and if a person falls below that, then they are in poverty. The problem with relative definitions in contrast is that they are always changing according to the society, the time, the social group and even according to the sociologist who is using the definition.

> *e* This is not a bad point. The candidate is questioning the reliability of the definition because its relativity means definitions are rarely stable or consistent across any period of time. A good range of examples, e.g. society, time, sociologists, is used to illustrate the point.

Secondly, studies by Breadline Britain and Townsend have used questionnaires to work out what people regard as basic needs, comforts and luxuries. The problem with surveys is that you cannot be sure people are telling the truth. People may decide to agree with the researcher regardless — Pawson calls this yea-saying. The response rates for questionnaires are also very poor.

> *e* The candidate has decided to focus quite generally on the merits of questionnaire surveys. This would have been fine if he or she had explicitly used 'relative poverty' to illustrate the points made. Unfortunately, although the points made are valid, they do not sufficiently address the question of poverty. Overall, the candidate identifies two problems, but whereas one is reasonably well developed, the other is not connected explicitly enough to poverty. The candidate would therefore score 8 out of a possible 12 marks.

(d) Poverty undermines the life chances of some social groups in several ways. For example, educational underachievement is probably due to cultural deprivation. J. W. B. Douglas found that working-class parents were less interested in their children's education compared with middle-class parents, whilst Wedge and Prosser found that children who lived in poverty were at least 2 years behind in terms of reading skills by the age of 9 compared with middle-class children. A recent study of kids in poverty claiming free school dinners suggests that such children were more likely to underachieve than other children.

> ✐ The candidate is right to focus on education but the material on parental attitudes is both very dated and not sufficiently linked to poverty. The material on Wedge and Prosser (which is also very dated) is more focused. The school dinners study is more contemporary but it needed to be referenced — who carried out the study?

Poverty can affect life chances in many ways. First, it can cause crime. Wilson, for example, argues that the increase in the crime rate is connected to the increase in poverty. Poverty also leads to increasing educational underachievement and decline in community. Lea and Young's left-realism theory of crime argues that the poor are more likely to experience relative deprivation and marginalisation and this may result in criminal and delinquent subcultures emerging in some inner-city areas.

> ✐ Some reasonable points are made in this paragraph but they are more theoretical than empirical. The studies quoted actually offer little evidence for their views.

There is evidence that poverty has a negative effect on family life. In particular, lone parents, most of whom are women, are much more likely to live in poverty than other types of family. For example, 75% of lone parents claim income support. Such one-parent families are more likely to live in poor housing conditions, especially overcrowded, privately rented accommodation. Limited state childcare provision makes it difficult for such mothers to find work, although the Labour government has attempted to create more flexible working conditions for them through the New Deal.

> ✐ This is a good paragraph focusing in some detail on the relationship between lone parents and poverty.

Finally, ethnic minorities also have their life chances affected by poverty. Brown notes how the quality of housing of black people tends to be poor, whereas Smith and Noble suggest that access to education for children from poor families is restricted by the expense of clothing and equipping children for school and the stigma attached to free school dinners. Smith and Noble identify several barriers to learning that negatively impact upon poor children at school. These include lack of finance, lack of health, lack of care, having insufficient funds to buy books or clothes for school attendance, and missing school because of illness. Such problems are doubled by the poverty faced by schools in urban areas, especially the limited funds allocated to them. The government is trying to target some of these areas through Education Action Zones.

✐ This paragraph makes some very good points because it is both focused on poverty and underpinned by sociological studies, i.e. Brown, Smith and Noble. Generally the response to part (d) demonstrates a detailed knowledge and understanding of a fairly wide range of evidence and concepts, especially in its latter stages. It would therefore score 18 marks out of a possible 22.

(e) The problem with poverty is that no one really knows how to define it and therefore measure it. Sociologists who believe in the absolute definition of poverty think it is no longer a major problem. Supporters of the relative definition of poverty believe that poverty still persists today and is, in fact, a major social problem.

✐ This introduction is a little tangential to the question. It does not really address sociological explanations of why poverty persists in the UK.

Oscar Lewis came up with the 'culture of poverty' idea. He said the reason why poverty continues is that poor people develop negative attitudes and values, which they pass on to their children. His studies of a Mexican village suggested that the rural poor live for today rather than planning for the future. They are apathetic and resigned to leading a life of poverty. They do not take an active part in society and they make little use of art galleries and museums. This culture of poverty prevents them from trying to escape from their situation and they pass these attitudes on to their children, and so the next generation also believes that there is little they can do to improve their situation.

✐ Although the candidate could have dropped the references to Mexico and the rural poor and adapted the material to the contemporary UK, this is a reasonably accurate summary of the culture of poverty thesis and deserves reward.

This culture of poverty idea is very similar to the 'poverty trap' explanation in Item B, although the poverty trap or cycle of poverty might have more to do with lack of economic support rather than attitudes.

✐ This is an evaluative paragraph in that it recognises a link between the two theories while acknowledging differences.

As Item B says, once people get into poverty it can be difficult to get out. Being poor can be quite expensive in that the costs are greater than the benefits, e.g. renting private property does not compare well with buying your own home. If you are poor, it may mean that your children's diet is poor, they may be more likely to get ill, they may take time off school, end up in the bottom streams and gain fewer qualifications. They may end up in a low-paid, unskilled job or unemployed. And the cycle begins again when they get married and have children. So both the culture of poverty and poverty trap ideas involve cycles within which people are trapped, although the culture of poverty suggests the poor are partly to blame whilst the poverty trap idea suggests that if people's living standards are raised, they could possibly escape from poverty.

e Despite its verbosity, this is not a bad paragraph. It illustrates the idea of the 'poverty trap' reasonably well, although it would have benefited from some reference to sociological studies. The end of the paragraph contains a focused, evaluative contrast between the culture of poverty thesis and the poverty trap idea. It also utilises the material in Item B well.

The culture of poverty idea is also very similar to the theory of an underclass, invented by Charles Murray. He argues that the poor do not want to work, that they supplement their income with crime and that they are not committed to family life. The underclass contains lots of unmarried mothers and absent fathers. These people deliberately live in poverty because they are happy to claim welfare benefits. They are conditioned by an over-generous welfare state to over-rely on hand-outs.

e This is a reasonably accurate summary of Murray's work but it needs to be linked more convincingly to 'persistence', i.e. the candidate could have said that the underclass is allegedly on the increase, and/or that the persistence of poverty is due to people's reluctance to lift themselves out of it.

Feminists partly agree with Murray. They argue that poverty is a problem because it has become feminised in recent years. One of the big reasons for this is increasing divorce which is causing one-parent families headed by females, and the rising number of single mothers. However, feminists argue that poverty is created by patriarchy, that is, the state is male-dominated and women are not seen as having a high priority. Moreover, women are increasingly found in low-skilled, low-paid and part-time work.

e Apart from the mistake of linking Murray to feminism, this is not a bad paragraph because it links increasing divorce (although it actually declined in the late 1990s), the rising number of women choosing to have children outside marriage, and the feminisation of low-skilled jobs to the persistence of poverty. The explanation of patriarchy, however, is a little simplistic and over-generalised.

Marxists suggest that poverty is caused by capitalism. They suggest that the bourgeoisie have a vested interest in poverty because it gives the impression that the capitalist system is just and the poor deserve their lot. Weberian sociologists agree and suggest that institutional racism also causes poverty for the same reasons.

e This is a vague paragraph which is theoretically quite weak. It is not clear how poverty functions to benefit the capitalist system or how institutional racism is linked to poverty.

Finally, poverty persists because of factors beyond people's control. Recession across the globe in places like Malaysia can have a negative economic impact in places like Newcastle or Coventry because many factories in the UK are owned by foreign companies which may shut them if their home economies go wrong. International recession can therefore be another reason why poverty persists in the UK.

e While the point about international recession is a valid one, at this level it really needs to be contextualised with the concept of globalisation and perhaps referenced in terms of a sociological study or theory. As it stands, this paragraph has a tendency towards generalised commentary rather than sociological analysis.

e Overall, this part (e) response demonstrates some knowledge and understanding of elements of the debate regarding the persistence of poverty, although it has a tendency to be brief and superficial. It is rather narrowly based, focusing on the culture of poverty, the underclass and the poverty trap rather than examining a range of theoretical explanations. For example, Marxist and Weberian explanations could have been pursued in more depth and detail. Evaluation tends to be by juxtaposition rather than focusing on the specific strengths and weaknesses of particular explanations, although there is some attempt at contrast. The candidate would therefore score 13 marks out of 20 for knowledge and understanding and 10 marks out of 24 for evaluation, making a total of 23 marks out of a possible 44.

Overall mark: 54/90

Task

Using the basic structure of this answer, rewrite part (e) so that it would gain higher marks. The following points will help you:

- Write an opening paragraph that sets the scene for the debate, i.e. outline the main arguments. There are essentially two broad positions: those explanations that blame the victims of poverty for their own situation (the underclass thesis of Murray, the welfare-dependency position of Marsland and the culture of poverty thesis), and those explanations that see social or structural factors as being responsible, such as influences beyond the control of the victims of poverty (Marxist, Weberian, feminists).
- Write a detailed paragraph on each of the three positions which make up the victim-blaming perspective, making sure that you acknowledge clearly the sociologists involved and address the idea of the persistence of poverty (e.g. Murray argues that poverty persists because the underclass is growing).
- Put together a detailed paragraph evaluating some of the main themes of the victim-blaming approach.
- Write four detailed paragraphs outlining those theories of poverty which blame the organisation of society. It is important to support these explanations with sociological studies and/or data, especially that relating to the distribution of wealth and income in the UK. Focus on the Marxist approach — how the organisation of capitalism might lead to situational constraints such as poverty; the Weberian

approach — how the organisation of the labour market and/or institutional racism might lead to poverty; and feminist approaches — how the treatment of women might lead to various types of poverty. Each of these explanations should be accompanied by some explicit evaluation of their positions.

- End with some sort of evaluative conclusion. In your view, which position is best supported by the evidence and why?

■ ■ ■

Answer to question 1: grade-A candidate

(a) First, one feature of poverty is the number of children, i.e. more than one in six children experience it. Over 2 million children lack necessities such as adequate clothing and a healthy diet according to the Joseph Rowntree Foundation.

e The candidate identifies clearly a feature relating to children and illustrates it with statistics taken from the item.

Second, over 9 million people cannot afford to heat their homes. This is going to affect some groups more than others, especially the elderly.

e The candidate identifies clearly the feature of being unable to afford adequate heating and interprets and analyses the data clearly. The response would earn the full 6 marks available.

(b) It is expensive to be poor because food costs a lot more for those who are unable to get to the large discount supermarkets which tend to be situated on the outskirts of towns. The poor are often forced to shop locally in shops which do not have a great range of healthy foods and which are often more expensive.

e This account identifies one of the reasons included in Item B in some detail.

Moreover, fuel such as gas, electricity and coal ends up costing more for the poor because they use more of it, as they cannot afford to have their lofts insulated or their homes double-glazed.

e Again, a clear identification is made with a detailed illustration. The candidate focuses succinctly on the relevant detail in Item B and would score the full 6 marks.

(c) Peter Townsend defines poverty as involuntary lack of access to the resources and lifestyles that communities take for granted as part of everyday life. However, as a concept 'relative deprivation' is difficult to operationalise and therefore measure because 'resources' and 'lifestyles', i.e. standards of living, are subject to social change. In other words, if we look at the experience of our own society, we can see that over the course of the century what were once luxuries have become comforts and even necessities. For example, most people would argue that a fridge, which was once regarded as a luxury item, is today a necessity. These changing definitions make it difficult to establish a norm. Studies of poverty using relative definitions and means of measurement are therefore difficult to compare

question

historically and need to be carried out fairly frequently in order to keep pace with social change.

> *e* The candidate identifies the 'relativity' of poverty as a problem in its own right in terms of operationalising and measuring poverty. The explanation is reasonably clear. It might have finished with the critique that only if everyone experiences the same standard of living (an idea rather than a realistic goal) will relative poverty ever be eradicated.

Sociologists such as Townsend and Mack and Lansley who have investigated the extent of poverty using relative definitions and tools of measurement, have experienced the problem of subjectivity, and consequently been accused of bias. For example, Townsend operationalised relative poverty by conducting a survey of 2,703 people in 1985–86. On the basis of the results, he compiled a deprivation index of items he thought symbolised poverty and concluded that people were in poverty if they lacked these items. Similarly, the Breadline Britain survey asked 1,174 people what they regarded to be necessities and compiled a list of poverty indicators. Mack and Lansley concluded that people were poor if they lacked three or more items from the list. However, both studies were criticised for coming up with arbitrary figures based on subjective judgements, i.e. why 12 or 3 items respectively? Despite attempts to produce public consensus on what is meant by necessities, the initial lists as represented by the questionnaire surveys were the products of the sociologists' subjective judgements rather than objective measurements of poverty.

> *e* The candidate identifies subjectivity as a problem facing sociologists investigating relative deprivation and explains this in the context of research by Townsend and Mack and Lansley. This is a sophisticated response which demonstrates a good understanding in its selection of focused, relevant, contextualised material. The candidate would therefore score 12 marks out of 12.

(d) It would be useful to begin by explaining which social groups are more likely to be found in poverty. Carey Oppenheim notes that certain groups face high risks of poverty. In particular, lone parent families (90% of which are headed by females), single pensioners (especially widows), the unemployed and adults in part-time and low-paid work are most susceptible to poverty. Although there are no poverty figures broken down by ethnic origin, African-Caribbeans, Bangladeshis and Pakistanis are more likely to be found in low-paid unskilled work or be unemployed and consequently more likely to be in poverty. What is clear is that all these groups are part of the working class. In fact, some sociologists have gone as far as suggesting that they are part of an underclass.

> *e* This is a good introduction which sets the scene by identifying the social groups most likely to be found in poverty. Note that the candidate works the concepts of gender, social class and ethnicity into the debate as well as acknowledging the underclass thesis.

The 1998 government consultation paper 'Our Healthier Nation' pointed out that the poorest in our society are hit harder than the well-off by most of the major causes of death. Poor people are ill more often and die sooner. Those who die youngest are those who live on benefits or low wages, in poor quality housing and who eat cheap, unhealthy food. The risk of dying before the age of five is more than twice as great for a child born into poverty than for a child from Social Class I. Moreover, the life expectancy of those higher up the social scale in profes-sional jobs has improved more than that of those lower down in unskilled jobs.

e Wider sociological knowledge about the relationship between poverty and health is accessed here. It is very easy in responses like this to list patterns and trends without acknowledging their source. This candidate has clearly referenced 'Our Healthier Nation' and covered a range of health inequalities.

Alcock identifies a range of different types of poverty and exclusion that are more likely to be experienced by ethnic minorities compared with white people. For example, ethnic minorities are more likely to be denied access to good quality private housing, to have poorer access to the welfare state and National Health Service and to have their poverty impact negatively on their children's chances of educational success.

e Good reference is made to the types of poverty experienced by ethnic minorities.

Some feminist sociologists, e.g. Glendinning and Millar, argue that in recent years we have seen the increasing feminisation of poverty in that the number of single mothers on benefits has increased in the past 20 years. Moreover, women are more likely than men to be low paid, in part-time work and, if elderly, are likely to lack occupational pensions and be widows. Cole notes that dependent wives are part of the 'hidden' poor, while Leavis and Piachard point out that women have always formed a majority of the poor.

e Good reference is made to another social group, women, although this part of the response does not make clear how poverty undermines their life chances.

The Joseph Rowntree Trust (1999) study of children growing up in low-income families focuses on the effects of poverty on their future economic and social fortunes. It found that having parents with low income during the socialisation years is a strong disadvantage, especially because such children learn to limit their expectations and ambitions for the future. They learn to accept less, such as wanting to do jobs that do not require qualifications. The report concludes that such children actually learn how to be poor. Consequently, poor children nearly always grow up into poor adults.

e The response ends with a reference to an empirical study which clearly links a social group, poor children, with general life chances (work, education etc).

e Overall, this candidate demonstrates a detailed knowledge and understanding of a wide range of concepts and empirical evidence. The answer covers a range of social groups and general life chances (e.g. work, health, housing, the welfare state), although the gender material could have been more clearly linked to effects. The candidate would score 20 out of a possible 22 marks for this response.

(e) There are two broad groups of sociological explanations for the persistence of poverty in the UK. The first is essentially cynical about the extent of that poverty, and is critical of the 'relative' deprivation indexes used by sociologists such as Townsend and Mack and Lansley. It is claimed that such ways of measuring poverty will always produce large numbers supposedly in poverty because there can never be a uniform standard of living experienced equally by all sections of society. In other words, there will always be a minority who go without compared with others. This approach, which is essentially a New Right perspective, claims that inequality has been mistaken for poverty, and living standards in the UK are such that no one need experience poverty. Consequently, many of those in 'poverty' are there voluntarily, because they are weak-willed or the culture they have been socialised into is inadequate. They are seen as part of an underclass which is over-dependent on the welfare state.

✍ This is a good start which attempts to set the scene of the debate. It identifies a New Right perspective which challenges the notion that poverty is a problem, and suggests that those claiming to be in poverty are the real problem.

In contrast with this view are empirical studies by Townsend etc. that suggest poverty is a major social problem today. For example, in 1990 Mack and Lansley's Breadline Britain survey claimed 11 million people in the UK were living in poverty. A number of sociological explanations originating in Marxist, Weberian, social democratic and feminist positions have suggested that poverty may have little to do with individuals or the culture to which they belong. Rather these explanations see poverty arising out of the social organisation of society, i.e. structural factors such as the changing nature of work, the dual labour market, globalisation, the distribution of wealth and income, patriarchy and racism are blamed for the persistence of poverty today.

✍ The other side of the argument is laid out clearly. The examiner can see that the candidate aims to cover a lot of ground in terms of both theory and concepts. This candidate needs to be aware that too much has been promised.

The New Right perspective takes a three-pronged approach to explaining why poverty persists. First, commentators such as Murray argue that many of the poor (although not all of them) belong to an underclass. Murray argues that it is not the fact of their poverty that is important. Rather it is the 'culture' of people claiming benefits that is the problem — this culture is made up of values and lifestyles that celebrate laziness, crime, immorality and welfare dependency, rather than individualism and self-reliance. In other words, this underclass has chosen poverty as a way of life. This is supported by those sociologists who argue that a 'culture of poverty' exists, i.e. that the poor significantly differ in their outlook and social characteristics from the rest of society. This second New Right view sees the poor as having developed a 'design for living' made up of deficient, fatalistic and often criminal value systems which are transmitted to the next generation, thus creating the potential for further delinquency and crime. A third New Right view, that of Marsland, considers that these processes are being made worse by an over-generous welfare state in which people are demotivated to take responsibility for their own welfare.

This is an extremely detailed section which weaves in three elements of the New Right approach to poverty. The candidate uses concepts clearly and includes elements of evaluation, such as indicating that not all the poor belong to the underclass.

This New Right perspective has similarities to the functionalist theory of stratification and inequality. Marsland, for example, argues that poverty has been confused with inequality by sociologists such as Townsend. Functionalists argue that inequality performs a positive function for capitalist society because it motivates all sections of the workforce who wish to avoid poverty. Poverty is the natural outcome of meritocracy. Those who fail do so because of individual or cultural weaknesses.

The candidate links New Right ideas to the functionalist theory of stratification well.

The evidence supporting the New Right view of poverty is mixed. There is little empirical evidence for the existence of an underclass and Murray, in particular, is guilty of confusing anecdote with fact. Marsland uses evidence selectively and ignores those groups which are poor but not dependent on the welfare state, such as the low paid. Research by Dear and Taylor-Gooby, Heath and Craine has found respectively that long-term benefit claimants do want to work, that people who claim income support share the same values as people who work, and that unemployed young people are ambitious for work. However, recent research by the Joseph Rowntree Foundation does indicate that poor children are taught to be poor and consequently are likely to be poor when they become adults.

Good use is made of empirical evidence to evaluate New Right approaches.

Some critical sociologists agree that an underclass has emerged in recent years but do not dwell on its supposed common and unified culture, as the New Right does. Rather the emphasis of these sociologists is on the reaction of the poor. It is suggested that the behaviour of the poor is often a realistic response to social influences or situational constraints beyond their control. For example, Craine found that in Manchester in the 1990s single parenthood for unemployed teenage girls, and street crime for teenage boys, were often the only realistic alternative to being unemployed and not having enough money, because welfare benefits were so low. Field notes that what unites this underclass is a common negative experience of the social change forced upon communities by government policies, global recession etc. In this sense, poverty is an unwelcome, involuntary experience.

🖉 This is an excellent evaluative section. It introduces an alternative perspective on the underclass and allows the candidate to progress smoothly to structural explanations of poverty.

Structural explanations for the persistence of poverty generally agree that the state of poverty is not the product of individuals or their culture. Social democratic accounts of poverty, for example, focus on the 'situational constraints' experienced by the poor. Poverty is seen as being caused by factors largely outside the control of the poor, such as the unemployment caused by economic and increasingly global recession, changes to the nature of work (especially the decline of the male-dominated primary and secondary sectors of industry), deskilling, downsizing, automation and the feminisation of the workforce. Moreover, such a perspective sees the welfare state as perpetuating poverty, not because benefits are too generous but because they are too mean.

🖉 The candidate makes an excellent link to changes in the workplace.

Other structural explanations, such as the Weberian-influenced dual labour market theory of Barron and Norris, focus on the organisation of the labour market. They argue that women and ethnic minority groups are more likely to experience poverty because they are part of a secondary labour market characterised by long periods of unemployment, low pay and insecure working conditions. They form part of this sector because of employer and trade union discrimination based on patriarchal and racist stereotyping. Moreover, a weak legal framework often fails to protect these groups against such discrimination and the resulting poverty.

🖉 A good link is made to a theory of employment, but it requires some evaluation.

Marxists see poverty as a natural outcome of the way capitalism is organised. In particular, class inequality and exploitation are the outcome of the fact that it is in the interests of the capitalist class to keep wages low in order to increase profits. Marxists also point to the unequal distribution of income and wealth in the UK as an explanation for the persistence of poverty. For example, they note that between 1977 and 1997, income inequality in the UK between the rich and the poor actually increased. The top 10% increased their income by 62% whilst the income of the poorest 10% fell by 17%. Moreover, although wealth in the hands of the top 10% has fallen over the course of the century, the majority of it is still in the hands of the wealthiest 25%. In other words, the extremely rich have transferred their wealth to the very rich rather than the poor. Consequently, Marxists argue that while few people continue to be very rich, a substantial part of society will continue to be very poor.

🖉 This is a good empirical section which uses evidence well to support the Marxist case.

Marxists note, like functionalists, that poverty has positive functions. However, these benefit the capitalist class rather than society as a whole. First, poverty functions to provide a reserve army of labour that can be hired in times of economic boom and fired in times of recession. Such a labour force provides the flexibility to deal with fluctuations in the capitalist system. Second, this reserve army of labour, made up of the poor in the form of women and ethnic minority workers, can be used to control the 'excessive' wage demands of the main workforce. It may even be used ideologically to divide and rule the working class in that workers may be encouraged to see the poor as a threat to their livelihoods, rather than the mismanagement of capitalism. In this sense, Marxists argue that capitalism has a vested interest in the persistence of poverty. This is why no real attempt has been made to eradicate the problem.

e The candidate offers a sophisticated account of poverty as an ideological weapon. However, the paragraph fails to evaluate Marxism.

Feminists argue that poverty is a natural outcome of a patriarchal system in which women are essentially second-class citizens confined primarily to family roles and denied access to well-paid jobs. However, despite the view that poverty has become feminised, there is evidence that opportunities in the job market are likely to benefit women more than men.

e This paragraph is a little generalised but contains relevant commentary and evaluation.

In conclusion, then, the empirical evidence probably supports structural rather than New Right theories for the persistence of poverty. While a minority of people probably do choose a life on benefits and avoid work, the evidence suggests that for the majority of the poor, especially the low paid, the elderly and lone parents, poverty is an involuntary experience caused by structural circumstances beyond their control.

e An attempt is made here to end with an evaluative conclusion, which is largely supported by the general content of the essay. Overall, the candidate demonstrates a detailed knowledge of a wide range of theories, evidence and concepts relevant to explaining the persistence of poverty. Most of the material is highly relevant to the question, which is addressed consistently throughout. The candidate would score 20 marks out of 20 for knowledge and understanding. Evaluation too is well developed and explicitly integrated throughout most of the essay. Critiques of structural theories are not as well developed as the critique of New Right theories, suggesting some imbalance. However, the candidate would score 21 marks out of a possible 24 for this skill, making a total of 41 out of 44 marks for part (e).

e This response is an example of a candidate who knows the material very well and is prepared to break out of a rehearsed answer and to make links across the 'Social Inequality and Difference' topic area to workplace inequality and theories of stratification, as well as incorporating issues relating to class, gender and ethnicity.

Overall mark: 85/90

Question Q2

Gender inequality in the workplace

Item A

Catherine Hakim (1995) argues that five feminist myths have been created about women's employment. For example, she takes issue with the feminist view that women's employment rates are rising. She argues that, although there has been an increase in the number of women working, the new jobs are generally part-time rather than full-time. She argues that women's full-time employment rate has generally remained static despite the social, economic and legislative changes that have taken place over the last 30 years. In addition, Hakim is critical of the feminist view that women's commitment to work is equal to that of men's and that the lack of childcare facilities is the main barrier to women going out to work. She argues that many women are happy with the traditional sexual division of labour and therefore choose to spend less time in paid employment.

Adapted from 'What do women want? Women, work and the Hakim debate', Jane Elliot, *Sociology Review*, April 1997.

Item B

Average hourly pay of full-time employees: by gender, Winter 1994–95 (GB £ per hour)

	Males	Females	Average pay
Black	7.01	6.71	6.88
Indian	8.01	5.75	7.12
Pakistani/Bangladeshi	6.87	4.78	6.43
White	8.34	6.59	7.73

Extracted from 'New approaches to social inequality' by Mark Kirby, *Sociology Review*, February 1999.

(a) Using only the information in Item A, identify two 'feminist myths' that Hakim claims have been invented about female employment. (6 marks)

(b) Identify two main differences in pay shown by the data in the table in Item B. (6 marks)

(c) Identify and explain two ways that sociologists might research 'women's commitment to work'. (12 marks)

(d) Using your wider sociological knowledge, outline the evidence for the view that patriarchy remains a feature of most aspects of UK society. (22 marks)

(e) Outline and assess sociological explanations of gender inequality in the workplace. (44 marks)

Total: 90 marks

Answer to question 2: grade-C candidate

(a) Hakim does not believe that many women are working full-time like feminists do. She argues that most women are working part-time.

> *This is not quite what Item A is saying, although the point made about part-time work is generally correct.*

She also thinks that women are happy with domestic work and prefer to do this rather than go to work.

> *This is not a clear or accurate interpretation of what Hakim says in Item A, although the core meaning is there. The candidate would score 4 out of a possible 6 marks for this response.*

(b) Black males earn more than black females, and Pakistani/Bangladeshi men earn over £2 per hour more than Pakistani/Bangladeshi females.

> *Whilst the information presented is accurate, the candidate misses the two main differences, i.e. the difference between males and females in general and the difference between whites and other ethnic minority groups. The candidate would therefore earn only 3 out of a possible 6 marks.*

(c) I would probably select a couple of women, one who is married with children and working part-time, and one who is married with children working full-time, and arrange to spend a week each shadowing them. This is a form of participant observation and should give me some insight into how committed to work they are. However, I would have to be aware that my presence might change their behaviour.

> *An inappropriate method for investigating women's commitment to work (i.e. attitudes) has been chosen, although the candidate does seem to recognise this. The candidate also fails to state how the women would be selected.*

I would also arrange for a postal questionnaire survey to be delivered to over 1,000 women with children who work full-time or part-time. I am not sure what sampling frame I could use — perhaps I could write to a company like a building society and request its help and use its personnel records. I would operationalise commitment by asking attitude questions on a scale of 1–5 about how they felt about going to work while having young children, whether they had postponed having children because they wanted a career etc. Postal surveys are notoriously bad for non-response rates so I would have to make sure that over 50% of my questionnaires came back so I could generalise to all working women with children.

> *The candidate does attempt to operationalise the concept of commitment. The response would have been enhanced by a brief discussion of how surveys might be advantageous compared with other methods for investigating this topic. The candidate touches upon sampling, representativeness and generalisability but the discussion is more evaluative than explanatory. The candidate would score 6 out*

of a possible 12 marks because only one appropriate method is identified and the explanation for that was in need of further development.

(d) One way in which you can tell patriarchy is still important is to look at studies of sexual behaviour. What studies like Sue Lees' 'Losing Out' tell us is that there are double standards operating when it comes to male and female sexual behaviour. What is considered positive behaviour by males, i.e. promiscuous sleeping around, is regarded as negative in females — they are likely to be negatively labelled, e.g. slag, slapper, tramp etc. for this behaviour. What this tells us is that the behaviour of girls is more closely socially controlled than the behaviour of boys. There have been cases where delinquent girls have been locked up by the courts because they have been regarded as too sexually experienced and therefore at risk.

e This is an interesting and fairly novel paragraph which demonstrates wider sociological knowledge. The candidate is accessing a classic sociological study, probably examined during the AS unit on The Individual and Society, to demonstrate how patriarchal attitudes might influence personal/sexual relationships.

We can also see patriarchy at work when we examine the criminal statistics. These show that most criminals are male. However, they might not be. Teenage girls commit as much crime as teenage boys according to self-report studies carried out by Campbell. However, they do not appear in the criminal statistics because police officers and the courts are patriarchal. Heidensohn's studies of the police suggest that male police officers treat female offenders in a paternalistic fashion. This means that female offenders are less likely to be arrested and are more likely to be cautioned because police officers do not believe females to be as criminal as males. Carlen too points out that male magistrates and judges are less inclined to imprison females who conform to a feminine stereotype in looks and dress, although those women who challenge conventional femininity, such as lesbians or women who abuse children, can expect to be treated very harshly.

e This section makes a very good synoptic link to crime and deviance that clearly outlines some aspects of the patriarchal nature of the criminal justice system, using relevant sociological studies.

Evidence is available in a range of other areas. Women do not earn as much as men at work and often experience sexual harassment and discrimination from employers. They also do well at school but do not do well at university. They face prejudice from the welfare state. They do not have the same pension rights as men, nor do doctors treat them very fairly, as Cartwright and O'Brien discovered. Finally, they often take most responsibility for children and housework within the family.

e This paragraph is trying to do too much. It takes pot-shots at five sociological areas but does not say anything convincing about any of them. It has a rather breathless, generalised feel and although some points are on the right track (women's earnings, discrimination, responsibility for children), there are mistakes in here too (e.g. Cartwright and O'Brien did not comment upon gender). It is too assertive, and each point needs more development and support from empirical, sociological studies.

ℓ Overall, however, this is not a bad attempt. The sections on sexual behaviour and crime deserve reward. The candidate would therefore score **17 out of 22 marks.**

(e) Women do not get the same opportunities as men in the workplace. The evidence suggests that they experience vertical segregation. This means that they are less likely than men to be found in skilled, highly paid jobs, e.g. there are lots of women school teachers but headteachers and principals are disproportionately male. Women experience what is called the glass ceiling effect. They can see the top jobs but they are denied access by men to those jobs. They also earn less money than men.

ℓ This is quite a good introduction despite its generalised character. It sets the scene for the debate. It needed to be more precise in its discussion of patterns and trends — what are the latest figures in terms of women's pay compared with that of men?

Sociological explanations of these trends tend to blame male employers. It has been said that employers are biased against women because women believe they are going to leave to have children and therefore waste expensive training. Burton and Norton said this was why women were not in the same employment sector as men. Employers did not trust them and as a result they were not given the same opportunities as males. However, I think this is a little dated nowadays. Girls do very well at school and there is evidence from higher education that a significant number of females are now going into professions which were once dominated by males. In addition, men's jobs have gone into decline because of the global recession and more jobs are available for women in the service sector. Management jobs in banks, building societies etc. are mainly taken up by men.

ℓ This is an interesting section which focuses in a very basic way on the dual labour market theory (read Barron and Norris for Burton and Norton). The ideas are on the right track but are on the verge of generalised commentary. The evaluation section is stronger, although it is undermined by its lack of sociological references.

In Item B a sociologist called Hakim points out that women choose to stay at home and have children. She argues that this is the biggest influence on why women cannot compete with men for the top jobs, promotion and pay. They quite simply do not want to because they are happy to settle down, get married and bring up children. Feminists violently disagree with Hakim. They point out that if you are brought up in a fiercely patriarchal society in which marriage and motherhood are stressed from childhood, choices are restricted because of the stigma and shame attached to being 'left on the shelf', and working mothers are blamed for delinquency.

ℓ This section is crudely expressed but sociologically focused. Hakim's ideas are presented with reasonable accuracy and the evaluation of her ideas is relevant.

Marxists too would criticise Hakim because she ignores the fact that capitalism needs a flexible and easily manipulated workforce. Marxist feminists like Benston point out that if women are seen as housewives first and wage-earners second, this means that when they do work and then are laid off, nobody really cares because they are going back to their 'proper' jobs in the home. In fact, capitalist ideology strongly implies that working mothers are more of a problem than mothers who are made redundant. In addition, if a woman is dependent on a husband's wage, it makes it easier for capitalists to control the male workforce who may be less willing to go on strike because they have so many dependants.

e Again, this is a rather crude and generalised account of Marxism, but it focuses in a basic fashion on some relevant aspects of the Marxist analysis, e.g. the flexible female workforce as the reserve army of labour, domestic labour etc. The lack of sociological studies (only Benston is cited) is a weakness.

Marxists, however, are criticised by feminists for ignoring the influence of patriarchy, which they see as being more important than capitalism. They argue that the family is a patriarchal institution which trains females via gender role socialisation to have lower aspirations when it comes to careers compared with males. However, this idea is rather deterministic — it sees gender role socialisation as a one-way process. In addition, the educational success of females in the past 20 years and the feminisation of the workforce suggest that feminism may now be a little dated. Females are obviously resisting the view that they should be passive and less ambitious than males.

e This is not a strong paragraph. Arguments around gender role socialisation are now very dated and they are no longer a central component of feminist analyses of inequality in the workplace. There is some acknowledgement of this in the rather underdeveloped evaluation.

Finally, Oakley argues that gender role socialisation results in women seeing the mother–housewife role as their priority at the expense of careers. This is not altogether different from the conclusion of Hakim who argues that gender inequality in the workplace is a result of women making rational choices about their futures. However, Oakley and Hakim differ in that Oakley sees this as negative whereas Hakim sees it as positive.

e Again, dated material is used. There is an attempt at an evaluative contrast but it is expressed in a basic fashion.

e Overall, this part (e) response demonstrates a reasonable knowledge of theory and concepts, although the candidate has a tendency to lapse into generalised commentary at the expense of analysis of sociological studies. The evaluation goes beyond juxtaposition — there are specific attempts to appraise the validity of theories such as Marxism, but these are often in need of greater detail and development. The candidate would therefore score 11 out of a possible 20 marks for knowledge and understanding and 13 out of a possible 24 marks for evaluation, making 24 marks out of 44.

Overall mark: 54/90

> **Task**
>
> Examine part (e) carefully and think about how you might rewrite it so that it would gain higher marks. The following points will help you.
>
> - Write an opening paragraph focusing on the facts of gender inequality in the workplace, using concepts such as vertical and horizontal segregation and the glass ceiling. Make sure you use contemporary material and reference your sources clearly.
> - Write 2–3 paragraphs exploring the dual labour market theory of Barron and Norris. Find other studies that support this theory to use as evidence. It is also important to evaluate the theory so you should acknowledge those studies which challenge key aspects of it.
> - Write 2–3 paragraphs explaining how Marxists explain gender inequality in the workplace. In particular, you should acknowledge the work of Benston, Braverman, Beechey, Hartmann and McDowell. Remember to evaluate aspects of these arguments.
> - Write 2–3 paragraphs on feminist approaches such as Crompton and Sanderson and Sylvia Walby. Make sure you clearly define the concept of patriarchy.
> - Write 1–2 paragraphs summarising and evaluating the work of Hakim.
> - Write a conclusion based on a reasoned appraisal of the evidence. What theoretical position is best supported by empirical studies to explain gender inequality in the workplace?

■ ■ ■

Answer to question 2: grade-A candidate

(a) Hakim is very critical of the idea that the workforce is becoming feminised because most of the jobs which are available for women, especially in the service sector, e.g. banks and building societies, are part-time rather than full-time. In fact, she argues that the number of women working full-time has hardly changed over the past 30 years.

> *e* This is a good example of how a candidate uses an existing stock of knowledge (here relating to the feminisation of the labour force, the service sector etc.) to enhance an interpretation of the material in the item.

Secondly, she disagrees with the feminist view that women are being held back in terms of job opportunities because the state has failed to provide free childcare facilities. Rather, she argues that women are more committed to looking after their children than pursuing careers. In other words, women's lack of opportunities is the product of making rational choices to stay at home and look after children.

⏚ This is a clear second identification, fully illustrated and using the material to good effect. The candidate would score the maximum 6 marks.

(b) First, we can see that whatever the ethnic group people belong to, males always earned more than women. In fact, all males earned over the average while all females earned under the average.

⏚ A difference between men and women across all ethnic groups is identified clearly. The reference to average pay reinforces the point.

A second difference is the fact that white male employees earned a good deal more than male employees from black, Indian and Pakistani/Bangladeshi backgrounds. In contrast, white women earned more than Indian and Pakistani/Bangladeshi women but slightly less than black women.

⏚ Another difference is clearly identified. The candidate would score the full 6 marks.

(c) One way in which sociologists might research 'women's commitment to work' might be to approach a service sector employer like a building society, which employs both full-time and part-time female workers. Once I had gained the cooperation of the company, I would use the personnel records as a sampling frame to randomly select a range of women to take part in structured interviews. It would be extremely important for those women to come from a variety of social backgrounds, e.g. married women with children working full-time, married women with children working part-time and single women. I would conduct the interviews away from the office and the home in order to minimise the effect of the workplace and the family, especially children, on the quality of responses. I would use female interviewers so that the interviewees might feel comfortable talking about female issues. The questions would mainly focus on how women interpreted their commitments at home, how these impacted upon choices in regard to work, and how they thought their employers interpreted their commitment to work.

⏚ This is quite a developed response. The candidate does not only tell us about using structured interviews, but gives appropriate context too in terms of how the research might be set up. The description of the research process could have been a little more detailed — it is unclear what sampling method would be used. It is also not clear what the strengths of structured interviews would be in this context.

I would also ask the women to keep diaries in which they should record their feelings and everyday experiences in regard to work, home and children. This would provide qualitative data and could be cross-referenced to support the findings of the structured interviews. The respondents should be guaranteed anonymity and confidentiality. This hopefully would encourage the female workers to be absolutely open and honest about work and family life. The combination of interviews and diaries may result in a triangulation of data, i.e. the reliability of the interviews can be tested by examining the findings of the diaries and vice versa.

e This is a good idea, although some brief reference to the strengths of diaries as a method in this context would have improved the marks. Good use of concepts is demonstrated. The candidate would score **9 marks out of 12**.

(d) The most obvious evidence that patriarchy remains a key feature of UK society is that relating to employment. Crompton and Le Feuvre (1996) argue that the most important factor determining whether a woman works or not is whether she has children, and especially the age of the youngest child. Men are not subject to such influences. Whether women work part-time or take time out of the labour market (which negatively affects their long-term promotion prospects compared with men) depends largely on social expectations. Patriarchal ideology expects that women should be primarily concerned with domestic and especially childcare commitments. Hartnett notes that employers may unconsciously discriminate against women if they have children because of the patriarchal belief that women will put their children before their commitment to work.

e This is a good start. The candidate focuses on how patriarchal beliefs or ideology shape our thinking and especially the thinking of employers about women, and how this results in women not enjoying the same life chances as men.

The result of such patriarchal thinking is that men and women have segregated experiences of work. Women are much more likely than men to work part-time (women constitute 84% of all part-time workers) and on average women only earn about 80% of what men earn. Moreover, women experience horizontal segregation, i.e. women mainly work with other women in the fields of clerical, secretarial, sales and personal service work whereas men dominate engineering, mechanics and agriculture. Women also experience vertical segregation — they are less likely than men to be found in top professional and managerial jobs.

e Good use of concepts is demonstrated in this section. The candidate identifies accurate evidence in the form of trends relating to vertical and horizontal segregation of work.

In the family, evidence relating to the patriarchal nature of society can be seen in the distribution of male and female labour in the home. The work of Leonard suggests that a gender role ideology determines whether housework and childcare is shared between men and women. Leonard notes that women who subscribe to a patriarchal gender role ideology see housework and childcare as an essential part of being a 'good wife and mother' and rarely complain about the non-participation of their partner. Leonard's empirical research into domestic labour indicates that few men share such tasks. As Leonard concludes, this division of labour suits men because it means that they can resist change.

e The candidate is using wider sociological knowledge to present evidence relating to gender roles within the family. Most candidates simply present statistical evidence of the inequality of domestic labour, but this candidate goes further by exploring research into the ideology of the home using the work of Madeleine Leonard.

In education too, we can see the influence of patriarchal attitudes. Despite improvements in female performance in education, there is evidence of continued gendered choices in subjects, especially at the further and higher education levels. Ann Colley's research indicates that such gendered choices may be partly responsible for creating horizontal segregation in the types of jobs men and women go into. Mirza's research suggests that the careers service and some teachers play a crucial role in pushing males and females towards gendered careers, which reproduce patriarchal divisions in the labour market.

> *e* Further and wider sociological knowledge relating to education is demonstrated here. The references to Colley and Mirza contextualise the response in terms of evidence.

There is also evidence suggesting gender divisions in mortality and morbidity. Women live longer than men (this also contributes to making female pensioners one group most at risk of poverty). However, evidence suggests that women record higher rates of illness than men, especially mental illness. Research by Hilary Graham points out that these higher rates of illness might be due to women bearing most of the responsibility for domestic labour and the physical and emotional care of their families, the dual burden of paid work and domestic labour, greater exposure to poverty etc. In fact, the research of Jesse Bernard led her to conclude that marriage makes women sick. According to Hicks, women face greater stress because they are likely to be caring for both children and other relatives such as ageing parents. There is some evidence that women may appear in the mental health statistics more than men because, as Busfield notes, male doctors are more likely to view certain types of behaviour as unfeminine and therefore unstable.

> *e* This is a very good section which is focused explicitly on evidence relating to death and illness. The references to Graham, Bernard and Hicks are excellent, as are the references to mental illness. Overall, the candidate focuses convincingly on a wide range of evidence and would be awarded the full 22 marks.

(e) As we have already seen, there is considerable evidence of gender inequality in the workplace relating to the distribution of full-time and part-time jobs, pay, and vertical and horizontal segregation. Such inequalities are generally connected to other types of gender inequality, especially within the family or health and welfare provision. For example, women tend to take responsibility for domestic labour and family health (while according a low priority to their own). Their lack of continuous work experience may mean that they lack welfare rights such as pensions that men take for granted.

> *e* A good introduction sets the scene without too much repetition of what has already been used in the part (d) response.

Moreover, it is important to note that gender interacts with ethnicity, and as we can see from Item B, women from ethnic minority groups are much more likely than white women to face inequalities in the labour market.

🖉 This is a good point which demonstrates that the candidate is thinking evaluatively.

Neo-Weberian accounts of gender inequality in the workplace have focused on the concepts of a dual labour market. Barron and Norris claim that two markets exist for labour: the primary sector, which is dominated by men and is made up of skilled well-paid jobs with long-term promotion paths clearly laid out; and the secondary labour market, which is dominated by women and ethnic minorities and is made up of unskilled, low-paid and insecure jobs. Hartnett argues that women are generally allocated to the secondary labour market because employers subscribe to patriarchal beliefs about women's commitment to their careers. Moreover, employers are supposedly less likely to invest in expensive training programmes for women who have not had children, believing that they are likely to interrupt their careers to have them. Caplow notes that child-rearing also interrupts the continuous service required for promotion. In addition, the legal framework supporting equal rights and pay in the UK, i.e. the Equal Opportunities Act and Equal Pay Act, is weakly enforced by the state. Consequently, this theory is sceptical that increased educational qualifications for females will make much difference to women's opportunities, because the glass ceiling is maintained by patriarchal ideology rather than women's lack of experience or ability.

🖉 This is an excellent paragraph which clearly and accurately explains the dual labour market theory.

However, Bradley is critical of Barron and Norris's theory because the evidence suggests that women can break into the primary sector, although it is unclear why women tend to occupy the bottom rungs of professional and managerial work.

🖉 Some specific evaluation is included but it requires further detail and development.

Feminist accounts of gender inequality at work vary, although all suggest that patriarchy — male domination of social structures, ideas and culture — plays a crucial role. For example, in the 1970s, liberal feminists, like Oakley, pointed to familistic ideology (Leonard calls it 'gender role ideology') which was influential in persuading both men and women that women's primary goal was the mother–housewife role. They would argue that such ideologies are still influential and can be seen in subject choice for females at the further and higher education levels.

🖉 This paragraph defines patriarchy succinctly and introduces its influence via 1970s liberal feminism, while acknowledging in an evaluative way that this theory may still be relevant today.

Marxist feminists insist that capitalism is responsible for gender inequalities in the workplace. Beechey argues that women form part of the 'reserve army of labour' which is essential to help capitalists manage the boom–bust nature of capitalism with minimum disruption and instability. Such a workforce is hired in times of economic expansion and fired in times of recession. However, capitalist ideology stresses that the 'natural' place for women is in the home, so therefore redundancy and unemployment for women provokes little protest from society. Moreover, domestic labour is crucial because it reproduces and maintains the future and present workforces respectively. However, this Marxist analysis has been criticised because it does not explain why there are men's jobs and women's jobs. It does not explain why women who do succeed in professional and management jobs can get only so far. Finally, it suggests that women's labour is cheaper than men's — if this was the case, surely the capitalist class would replace male labour with cheaper female labour?

This is another excellent summary with an evaluative commentary.

Some Marxists, such as Hartmann, have attempted to suggest that patriarchy and capitalism operate together to oppress women. Hartmann notes that low pay operates to keep women economically dependent upon men, which encourages marriage and domestic labour. This further benefits men by supporting their careers while further weakening women's position in the labour market because they are unavailable to take paid work.

This is a good paragraph that makes synoptic links between work and family.

Walby has probably constructed the most convincing explanations of gender inequalities at work, using the triple systems approach. She notes that patriarchy has three elements to it: subordination or unequal relations between the sexes; oppression, i.e. discrimination; and exploitation, i.e. women gain little reward for their labour. Walby argues that the family is over-played as the major source of patriarchy. Rather she notes that many households (and therefore men in their roles as husbands or partners) depend upon women's participation in the labour force for financial stability. She therefore argues that the causes of women's inequality in the labour market are not the roles women play within the family. Instead she blames employers who have organised the workforce into full-time and part-time work in order to exploit all workers (not just women) more effectively and flexibly in response to the changing nature of work. Moreover, she points out that gender inequality is maintained by the state, which has been slow to respond to social change.

Another excellent summary of a complex theory is given.

Finally, Hakim has been critical of feminist theories of workplace inequality. She claims that they neglect the fact that women are actively engaged in making rational choices about their futures. To put it simply, she argues that women are not as committed to work and careers as men because women give priority to marriage and childcare. She suggests that feminism has been allowed to devalue family life. Inequality in the workplace, therefore, is not caused by patriarchy but by intelligent women choosing to reject careers. Unsurprisingly, feminists have been unwilling to accept this position and Crompton, in particular, has pointed out that women do not make choices in a cultural vacuum. Rather, the choices women have are constrained by their lack of power and resources relative to those held by men. It could be argued that ethnic minority women are similarly constrained. They cannot make the same decisions about work and family as white women, as they may be constrained by culture, religion and racism.

e This is an excellent evaluative paragraph which covers Hakim's critique of feminism but also incorporates a feminist response to her ideas, plus an evaluative comment about women from ethnic minority backgrounds.

e Overall, this is a high-quality response to the question. It covers a wide range of complex theoretical material clearly and accurately. It has an evaluative tone throughout and addresses the specifics of key issues in an analytical way. Although the candidate might have evaluated issues of social class (e.g. feminism assumes a universal gender experience at times and fails to distinguish between working-class and middle-class gendered experience) and ethnicity more deeply (some of the theories discussed take analysis of women and ethnicity a step further), this is still a first-class response. The candidate would be awarded the full 20 marks for knowledge and understanding, and 21 out of 24 marks for evaluation, making 41 out of 44.

Overall mark: 84/90

Changes in the class structure

Item A

Predictions based on present trends suggest that in countries such as Britain, manufacturing will cease to be a significant source of employment. If roughly 35% of the labour force were engaged in manufacturing occupations in the late 1970s, by the year 2010 the comparable figure will be about 15%. Trends also indicate that developments in information technology will increase the number of low-paid and low-skilled jobs in the UK, such as those found in call centres. Many of these new jobs are part-time and occupied by women. In particular, call centres constitute one of the major areas for economic growth. Call centres have emerged directly as a result of developments in information technology. Essentially they provide services over the telephone, which can range from booking airline tickets to the provision of financial services, such as banking, insurance and personal finance.

Adapted from 'The future of work', Richard Scase, *Sociology Review*, November 1998.

Item B

Braverman argues that in the late twentieth century, work has undergone a process of deskilling in that complex skills have been fragmented into routine simple tasks. Consequently, the status of such jobs has experienced decline. In particular, he suggests that this deskilling process has extended from the factory into white-collar work. Office work has become more routine, involves less decision-making and responsibility, is more subject to managerial control and takes place in organisations that are larger and more bureaucratised than ever. In particular, he notes that mechanisation has impacted negatively on the work situation of routine white-collar workers. The computer may represent a particularly dramatic way of reorganising office work but other machines have also replaced particular traditional skills. Duplicators, photocopiers, dictating and addressing machines and, more recently, word processors have produced conditions of work similar to those of factory workers. Braverman concludes, then, that the class boundary between the middle class and working classes is disappearing because lower middle-class white-collar workers are experiencing proletarianisation. However, others suggest that the material and cultural differences that characterise the relationship between the working classes and the middle classes remain firmly in place.

Adapted from Abercrombie, N. and Warde, A. (2000) *Contemporary British Society* (3rd edn.), Polity.

(a) Using only the information in Item A, identify two reasons why the nature of work is changing in the UK. *(6 marks)*

(b) Identify two aspects of deskilling found in routine white-collar work as identified in Item B. *(6 marks)*

(c) Identify and explain one strength and one weakness of using covert participant observation to investigate working conditions in call centres. *(12 marks)*

(d) Using your wider sociological knowledge, outline the evidence that challenges the view that 'we are all middle class now'. *(22 marks)*

(e) Outline and assess sociological explanations of the view that the changing nature of employment is having significant effects on class boundaries. *(44 marks)*

Total: 90 marks

■ ■ ■

Answer to question 3: grade-A candidate

(a) Item A suggests that the nature of work is changing because manufacturing industry is in decline. For example, in the late 1970s about 35% of the labour force was employed in factories, while by 2010 it is predicted that this figure will fall to 15%.

> *℮* One reason is identified clearly, using the material in Item A to full effect. Note that the candidate has resisted the temptation to offer an explanation for this trend.

Secondly, another reason why the nature of work has changed is because of the introduction of information technology. Computers have revolutionised working practices as can be seen in the rapid growth in call centres in recent years, which have encouraged part-time work and the feminisation of the service sector.

> *℮* The candidate identifies clearly another reason using both Item A and a stock of sociological knowledge. The candidate would therefore be awarded the full 6 marks.

(b) One aspect of the deskilling process is the automation that drives it forward. The computer, in particular, and other office machines such as word processors have led to traditional skills such as book-keeping and secretarial work being broken down into simple, routine, repetitive tasks.

> *℮* Automation is identified and illustrated clearly.

Secondly, deskilling has led to control over the work process being further taken away from workers. This process started with assembly-line production in factories, but has now been extended to white-collar work. Deskilling means that office workers now expect more routine, less scope for making decisions on their own and more managerial and bureaucratic control.

> *℮* This is a detailed illustration of lack of power and control as an aspect of deskilling. The candidate would be awarded the full 6 marks.

(c) One strength of using covert observation to investigate working conditions in a call centre is that people's behaviour is likely to remain natural. If people know that a sociologist is present, then the quality of their behaviour is likely to change. For example, employees are likely to suffer from the Hawthorne or observer effect, i.e. they are likely to modify their behaviour in order to impress the sociologist because they may suspect the investigator to be an agent of the employer. Consequently, the observation is unlikely to accumulate valid data because employee behaviour is artificial. Similarly, supervisors might also view the sociologist's presence with some suspicion and change their behaviour. Although the researcher can never be quite sure that a covert presence is not having some effect upon the people he or she is researching, the fact that people do not know sociological research is being conducted can reduce potential problems and increase the validity of the data gathered.

> ✏ This is an intelligent and conceptually confident discussion of why covert observation might be a strength. Note how the examples relate specifically to call centres. This is important in order to pick up all the marks available.

A weakness of using covert observation in a call centre is that the nature of working practices in such organisations means that you do not have very much contact or interaction with your fellow employees. The likelihood is that you will be restricted to a booth and spend most of your working hours talking on the telephone. Walkabouts are usually prohibited and breaks are short, infrequent and staggered so that people are always manning the phones. The only time a sociologist might get to observe what is going on is the lunch break, which may not give much valid insight into the working conditions. Other methods such as interviewing ex-call centre staff might prove more useful.

> ✏ This is a flexible response which applies sociological knowledge of call centres and covert observation very well to the research context. Overall, this candidate demonstrates a very keen knowledge of methods and observation and would be awarded the full 12 marks.

(d) The view that we are all middle class now was expressed by Tony Blair a few years ago. However, the evidence does not support Blair's view. If it did, it would show that people from all social backgrounds were experiencing similar standards of living and opportunities. This is not the case. The evidence quite clearly challenges Blair's view and shows that class differences are still as acute as they were 50 years ago and that poverty in the UK is a major problem.

> ✏ This is a good introduction which sets the scene for examining the evidence.

Income and wealth statistics are a good place to start. Fifty years ago, there were great inequalities in the distribution of wealth and income across social groups in the UK. The top 1% of the population owned over 40% of wealth in 1950. If we look at their share today, we can see a marked decline. They only owned about 18% in 2000. This is still a substantial inequality. In fact, we can see that what the wealthy seem to have done over the years is to transfer their wealth to other family members via trust funds. For example, in 2000, the top 10% of the wealthy owned nearly half of all wealth in the UK. This is hardly evidence of equality. Similarly, Will Hutton points out that in terms of income, the top 10% have actually got richer in the past 20 years while the bottom 10% have actually got poorer.

e There is excellent use of wealth and income statistics and the study by Hutton, but the candidate now needs to demonstrate wider sociological knowledge.

Another area of social life which indicates that class inequalities are actually growing is health. There is no doubt that for all sections of the population health has got better in that life expectancy has increased and all people are less likely to die of a range of diseases. However, the gap between middle-class and working-class life expectancy has widened. Members of the working class are living longer but not as long as those of the middle class. Moreover, the numbers of middle-class people surviving cancer and heart disease has increased at a much faster pace than the number of working-class people surviving such diseases.

e Some relevant trends are highlighted and these count as evidence, but the candidate needs to focus on sociological studies as well in order to pick up all potential marks.

Wilkinson's study of class-based diet and exercise indicates some cultural differences between members of the working class and middle class, which may be part of the cause of the differences in mortality and illness. For example, Wilkinson notes that middle-class people are more aware of health as an issue and are willing to seek advice from doctors in order to keep fit and healthy. They are more likely to take up active sports such as squash, tennis and golf. They also eat more healthily and think more about having a nutritious and fat-free diet. They are less likely to smoke and drink to excess too. Working-class people, on the other hand, are less likely to take an interest in how their lifestyle may be impacting upon their health. They are less likely to visit doctors for check-ups and more likely to indulge in fatty diets, especially those revolving around fast food. However, Wilkinson does note that these class-based trends are not exclusively cultural in origin. He points out that culture is to a great extent shaped by economic circumstances, and he concludes that poor health has more to do with inequalities in income and wealth than cultural differences in behaviour.

e This is an excellent section which identifies a good range of class-based differences in behaviour which may affect health, and uses the study of Wilkinson to explore some class-based explanations.

We can see that class is important in terms of the quality of family life and how it impacts upon education and achievement. For example, it is a fact that middle-class children achieve higher levels of education than working-class children. Some sociologists, particular Bourdieu and Bernstein, have noted that the habitus of middle-class families is advantageous because it equips their children with ways of seeing the world, ways of articulating the world and aspirations which make the passage through education smoother (especially at the further and higher levels). This habitus therefore provides these children with cultural and economic capital. Evidence from studies of the middle class, e.g. by Savage, and studies of middle-class girls in private education, e.g. by Charlotte Butler, indicate that middle-class children take for granted that they will go on to university and achieve professional and managerial occupational roles. These aspirations are generally absent from working-class children, who come from families with no experience of further and higher education. A recent study of poverty by the Joseph Rowntree Foundation found that children brought up in poverty had very low aspirations in terms of their education. The notion of taking A-levels and going to university was alien to them.

> This is another excellent and perceptive section which at first seems as if it might be over-reliant on theory but compensates well by focusing on evidence from Savage, Butler and the Joseph Rowntree Foundation.

> Overall, this candidate has demonstrated a wide-ranging knowledge of class differences and has very intelligently challenged the notion that the UK is a classless society. The candidate focuses on evidence throughout and understands this debate well. The response would be awarded the full 22 marks.

(e) The nature of work in the UK has undergone great change in the past 30 years. In particular, the primary and secondary sectors of the economy have gone into decline. Heavy industries such as coal-mining and manufacturing or factory work have experienced recession because raw materials can be extracted and goods such as cars manufactured more cheaply in other parts of the world. Male manual work has consequently gone into decline.

> The candidate has decided, quite rightly, to focus on the changes to employment before focusing on their effects upon class boundaries.

However, we can also see that the tertiary or service sector of the economy — those jobs organised around the public sector (education, welfare etc.), personal services (such as retail) and finance — has expanded dramatically. The expansion of mass education, and especially the increase in people going into higher education, has meant that a well-educated and qualified workforce is available to take on these jobs. Many of the jobs available in this sector have been for women, especially in part-time work.

> The candidate contrasts the decline of the traditional sectors of work with the rise of the service sector and notes the feminisation of the labour force, although this is qualified with the reference to part-time work.

It is argued that Fordist working practices, i.e. fragmented, simple, routine and boring tasks characterised by assembly line production, deskilling and controlled by a hierarchical management, have been replaced by robot technology and computers. The jobs that exist in the postindustrial world are characterised by 'functional flexibility', i.e. the modern worker is likely to be multiskilled, to be more adaptable and flexible and to be more motivated and committed. The relationship between workers and management has also allegedly changed. The formerly conflict-orientated relationships of industrial society have been replaced with relationships between workers and bosses built on consensus and cooperation. However, it is also noted that work is no longer characterised by the stability of long-term security in the form of full-time contracts. Work in the postindustrial age is likely to take the form of contracting out, to be temporary or part-time, and even casual.

✐ The candidate contrasts the nature of work in the industrial age with the nature of work in the postindustrial age successfully, and begins to touch upon the implications for the class structure.

However, critics of the postindustrial argument claim that the case for de-industrialisation has been overstated. Manufacturing still makes up a major part of the economy and manual work still takes up a substantial part of the labour force. Moreover, the growth in the service sector has been long-standing — it is not a recent event and consequently employment in that sector has always been important. Marxists argue that so called post-Fordist techniques are merely new means by which the labour force is exploited.

✐ There is some sustained and pertinent evaluation here, which implies that as far as the class structure is concerned little has changed.

So what has changed? There are a number of trends that we can be reasonably sure of. First, the process of deskilling and automation continues. In fact, some Marxists, particularly Braverman, argue that routine white-collar workers are no longer members of the middle class because employers are increasingly using technology, especially computers, to break down complex white-collar skills such as book-keeping into simple routine tasks, in an attempt to increase output, maximise efficiency and reduce costs. These developments have been accompanied by the parallel development of feminising the white-collar workforce, because female workers are cheaper than male employees and are seen by employers to be more adaptable and flexible. Braverman concludes that white-collar workers have therefore been subjected to a process he calls 'proletarianisation', i.e. they have lost the social and economic advantages that they traditionally enjoyed over manual workers. He argues that they now have similar conditions of work and pay to blue-collar workers. A good example of this type of deskilling is the growth of call centres, which are not dissimilar in their workplace characteristics from factory assembly lines. White-collar workers in call centres are strictly controlled by management, have to take a set number of calls a day and keep to strict rules in the way they take those calls, and are allowed to take toilet and lunch breaks only at times set by management.

e This is a good section focusing on deskilling and proletarianisation, which uses the example of call centres well to illustrate the Marxist case. The consequences for class boundaries are very clearly laid out.

However, research by Devine suggests that Braverman may have overstated the case for proletarianisation, because her research indicates that distinct cultural differences in terms of values, lifestyles and political attitudes still exist between manual workers and white-collar workers. Moreover, white-collar workers still enjoy advantages over manual workers in terms of working conditions. They have access to flexitime, fringe benefits, longer holidays and safer working conditions.

e This is a good evaluation of the Braverman argument.

Despite our scepticism in regard to proletarianisation, it can be safely assumed that deskilling is an ongoing process. Evidence also indicates that post-Fordists have overstated the concepts of upskilling and multiskilling. Critics of multiskilling have suggested that most workers, whether they are in blue-collar or white-collar work, have probably experienced multitasking, i.e. the volume of their work has probably increased while their conditions in terms of pay and security have got worse. There is evidence too in all sectors of work that the number of full-time workers on permanent contracts is on the decline. Instead, the economy is experiencing a casualisation of labour, i.e. more people are being hired on temporary contracts for shorter periods of time with few employment rights. In recent years, the recession has led to the downsizing of the financial sector and many managers have lost their jobs.

e This section is attempting to identify trends in regard to the changing nature of employment which might be impacting on class boundaries. This is quite a difficult task but the candidate has been reasonably successful.

There are a number of implications for class resulting from the above trends. Will Hutton argues that the traditional class categories (i.e. the Registrar-General's five-class categorisation) are now a little dated in the light of these changes. He argues that society is now split into a 30–30–40 society in that 30% of people are disadvantaged because they are unemployed and in poverty, 30% are marginalised and insecure because they are employed temporarily either part-time or casually, and 40% are privileged by having full-time, reasonably secure jobs.

e This is an excellent use of Hutton to illustrate the changing nature of employment and its effect upon social categories.

Even the authorities that define and measure class have adopted a new type of class categorisation to reflect these changes. The NS–SEC system of classifying occupations now takes into account people's employment relations, e.g. whether they work full-time or part-time, and market conditions, e.g. their salaries, promotion prospects and the degree of control they exercise over their work. This scale of occupations no longer divides workers along manual and non-manual lines.

questions & answers

e There is good use of the new social class scales to illustrate the changing nature of work.

Despite these changes to the nature of work, there are sociologists who argue that very little has changed in terms of class boundaries. Sociologists like Savage argue that non-manual workers have become the majority occupational group in the workforce (at 67%). He notes that most of the groups or class fractions that make up this group still continue to enjoy considerable material and cultural advantages over other occupational groups. Professionals, in particular, have consolidated their class position, and through habitus and cultural capital are able to pass on their advantages to their children. Savage does acknowledge that three middle-class fractions have experienced some insecurity in recent years — the self-employed, managers and white-collar workers — but all continue, as Devine notes, to enjoy greater life chances than the working class.

e The candidate examines the other side of the coin, i.e. the view that there has been little change.

Marxists too, despite Braverman's thesis, argue that the position of the working class has hardly changed. The changes described above — deskilling, casualisation etc. — are merely part of the ongoing exploitative nature of capitalism and are likely to drive the working class closer still to pauperisation and consciousness as a class for itself. Critics, such as feminists, however, argue that Marxists are ignoring the crisis of masculinity that has been created by the fact that male jobs are being increasingly replaced by jobs for females. Some sociologists argue that this is the real problem created by the changing nature of work, because it is resulting in a mass of disaffected and alienated boys and men characterised by lack of qualifications and the potential for crime, urban disorder and violence against women.

e The candidate ends with a brief discussion of the traditional Marxist view and a critique focusing perceptively on the crisis in masculinity.

e Overall, this is a very good response. It identifies a range of possible changes in the way work is organised and shows a wide-ranging and detailed knowledge and understanding of the implications for class-boundary debates. This is an extremely wide debate and it is probably best to focus on some aspects of it in detail rather than try to deal with all aspects in a superficial fashion. This candidate did just this by deciding to focus on proleterianisation, the work of Hutton and the NS-SEC. The candidate would therefore be awarded 18 out of 20 marks for knowledge and understanding. Evaluation is generally excellent, although it could be argued that some theories, especially Marxism, were not subjected to a sustained analysis. The candidate would score 22 marks out of 24 for this skill, making a total of 40 marks out of a possible 44 for part (e).

Overall mark: 86/90

Q4

Ethnic minority inequalities in employment

Item A

Job levels of men by socioeconomic group

	Percentage			
	White	**African-Caribbean**	**Indian**	**Pakistani**
Prof/managers/employers	30	14	25	19
Intermediate and junior non-manual	18	19	20	13
Skilled manual and foreman	36	39	31	46
Semi-skilled manual	11	22	16	18
Unskilled	3	6	5	3
Total non-manual	**48**	**33**	**45**	**32**
Total manual	**50**	**67**	**54**	**67**

Source: Modood 1997, extracted from Mason, D. (2000), p. 49, *Race and Ethnicity in Modern Britain,* 2nd edition, Oxford University Press.

Item B

Studies of discrimination in employment have investigated the extent of different treatment of majority and minority ethnic groups. One way of establishing the degree of discrimination in employment is to arrange for equally qualified white and minority workers to apply for the same job. These experiments generally show that there is discrimination against ethnic minority candidates in the sense that the minority actor is not given the job, or is told it is filled, while the similarly qualified white actor is offered the job. Other sociologists have blamed the institutional racism apparent within the education system, which prevents some ethnic minority groups making the best of their abilities and talents. However, discrimination on the grounds of colour or ethnicity is not a sufficient explanation of the persistence of racial disadvantage. It can be argued that the greatest disadvantage is caused by structural changes in employment opportunities such as the decline of the manufacturing sector.

Source: Mason, D. (2000), p. 49, *Race and Ethnicity in Modern Britain,* 2nd edition, Oxford University Press.

(a) **Using only the information in Item A, identify two major differences in job levels between ethnic minority groups.** (6 marks)

(b) Identify *two* reasons why ethnic minority groups experience racial disadvantage in employment according to Item B. (6 marks)

(c) Identify and explain *two* problems facing sociologists who use experiments to research racial discrimination in employment. (12 marks)

(d) Using your wider sociological knowledge, outline the evidence for the view that racism is a common experience in UK society. (22 marks)

(e) Outline and assess sociological explanations of ethnic minority inequalities in employment. (44 marks)

Total: 90 marks

■ ■ ■

Answer to question 4: grade-A candidate

(a) First, we can see that white people are more likely than any other group to be employed in non-manual work (48%), although Indians are not far behind (45%). The other minority groups are overwhelmingly likely to be found in manual jobs. Second, a greater proportion of whites are employed in professional and managerial jobs (30%) whereas only a small proportion of African-Caribbeans are employed in this kind of work (14%).

e Two clear differences are identified in terms of scale. The candidate was aware that these trends are not broad and noted the similarity between whites and Indians in regard to non-manual work. The candidate would be awarded the full 6 marks.

(b) One reason members of ethnic minority groups may experience racial disadvantage in employment is discrimination. Brown conducted experiments using English, Asian and European actors. Application forms were sent to companies which described Asian and English applicants with exactly the same characteristics as far as qualifications, skill levels and experience were concerned. However, English applicants found themselves disproportionately invited for interview compared with Asian applicants. In Item B, we see white actors being offered jobs whilst similarly qualified black actors are told the same jobs have been filled.

e The candidate uses knowledge of Brown's study to supplement interpretation of the data in Item A. However, too much detail is given for a question on which only 5 minutes should be spent.

Another reason ethnic minorities may be experiencing racial disadvantage is that they may be leaving education with few qualifications to compete in the job market because of institutional racism embedded in the education system. Studies such as Mirza, Fuller, Troyna etc. have all demonstrated that some teachers may label African-Caribbean youth negatively and allocate them to bottom streams. A self-fulfilling prophecy may occur if these pupils organise themselves into anti-school cultures.

e A second reason is identified and well illustrated. The candidate identifies two reasons and would be awarded the full 6 marks.

(c) The first big problem is that sociologists who conduct such experiments can never be sure that the variable they are interested in — in this case, racial discrimination — is the one that is causing the employer behaviour. The problem with experiments of this type is that it is almost impossible to isolate one particular variable — there are literally hundreds affecting any one social situation. For example, an employer might be turning down applicants with Asian names because the workforce is overwhelmingly white and he or she feels that an Asian worker might be at risk of racial harassment.

Secondly, the evidence in terms of Asian applicants being turned down might indicate racial discrimination but does not prove it. Such 'evidence' is speculative. We can never know the motives of an employer unless we use a research tool which allows us directly to access his or her interpretation of the situation.

> ✐ This is a difficult question but the candidate thinks it through carefully and constructs two perceptive criticisms of experiments. The candidate would be awarded the full 12 marks.

(d) Racism is a term that covers a wide range of discriminatory practices and negative beliefs, attitudes and stereotypes, i.e. prejudice, which result in black people having poorer jobs, health, education, housing and life chances compared with the white majority.

> ✐ The candidate begins with a definition of the components of racism, although the answer needs to move on to examine the evidence as soon as possible.

Studies of racial prejudice in the UK suggest that a substantial minority of white people admit to being prejudiced against black people. For example, a European Union-wide survey conducted in 1997 found that one in three Britons (32%) believed themselves to be very racist (8%) or quite racist (24%).

> ✐ This is a good, reasonably contemporary example.

Studies of mass media content suggest a racist agenda, especially in the tabloid press. Content analysis studies, e.g. Van Dijk, Gordon and Rosenberg, Hartmann and Husband, suggest that black people are often stereotyped as a threat to white society in terms of immigration, crime, drugs, welfare dependency etc. It is believed that the media transmit racist myths and fears and, on occasion, create moral panics about ethnic minorities which reinforce prejudice and may even create the climate for racial harassment, name-calling and violence.

> ✐ The candidate is using wider sociological knowledge well to access synoptic material from AS study of the mass media.

There is evidence, as stated in Item B, of employer discrimination against black people in terms of jobs. Brown surveyed over 5,000 black people and concluded that many of his sample had experienced discrimination in terms of job applications, but also from landlords, building societies, council housing departments etc. when searching for somewhere to live. Such discrimination probably explains why black people are found in disproportionate numbers in low-skilled manual work and privately rented accommodation.

This paragraph is in danger of over-generalising the experience of black people. However, the Brown research is a good piece of evidence to cite and goes beyond the Social Inequality and Difference unit by focusing on housing.

The Home Office has recently highlighted the problem of racial attacks in our society, in the light of the Stephen Lawrence Enquiry. It is estimated by the government that, compared with whites, Asians are 50 times and African-Caribbeans 36 times more likely to be victims of a racially motivated attack in the UK. Figures suggest 8,000 reported racial attacks in the UK every year, but this is likely to be an underestimate.

This is a good contemporary reference to the Stephen Lawrence Enquiry, and again there is evidence of wider sociological knowledge accessing material about crime and deviance.

There is some evidence of police racism. The Stephen Lawrence Enquiry accused the police of institutional racism. This is where racism is embedded, perhaps unconsciously, in the rules, regulations and everyday practices of an organisation. Studies of police forces and officers on the beat, e.g. Smith and Grey, and Holdaway, have indicated that some police officers do operate with negative stereotypes of black people and assume that their behaviour is more suspicious or criminal than that of white people's.

The candidate extends the debate to include 'institutional racism', which is defined clearly and linked to evidence regarding police behaviour.

Finally, some sociologists have accused the education system in the UK of institutional racism too. Wright's ethnographic study of four inner-city primary schools suggests that teachers exclude Asian children from group discussions because they assume they have a poor command of English, while the same teachers assume that African-Caribbean boys are disruptive and difficult to deal with. These negative views result in African-Caribbean boys being treated more harshly. Such children, argued Wright, develop low self-esteem or become hostile to the classroom and this may result in educational underachievement. Other studies, e.g. the Swann Report, have suggested that the knowledge taught in schools (the national curriculum) and teaching methods are ethnocentric — they reflect white rather than black experience and therefore 'turn off' black children from the learning process.

This is another excellent example of wider sociological knowledge. This section focuses clearly on evidence in its referencing of Wright and Swann.

Overall, the candidate demonstrates an excellent and perceptive wider sociological understanding, using material which is clearly focused on evidence relating to education, crime and deviance, housing, racial attacks, mass media representations,

general prejudice and jobs. A response of this quality would score the full 22 marks for knowledge and understanding.

(e) The evidence very clearly indicates that there are ethnic inequalities in employment. However, these affect some ethnic minority groups more than others. If we examine unemployment, we can see that in 1995 white men experienced an unemployment rate of 8% compared with 18% for Pakistani/Bangladeshi men and 21% for African-Caribbean men. Unemployment is particularly bad for young members of ethnic minorities. For example, Scarman estimated that over 50% of African-Caribbeans aged 16–24 were unemployed in the early 1980s, while in the early 1990s at least twice the number of 16–24-year-old African-Caribbeans were unemployed compared with whites of the same age. Ouseley estimates that in London alone, 62% of young black males are unemployed.

e The candidate sets the scene by giving us a flavour of inequalities in ethnic minority employment before examining the explanations. Note too how the candidate has differentiated between different ethnic minority groups.

When we come to look at those in employment, we can see distinct differences in skill levels and pay. Official Labour Force Surveys indicate that in 1995, only 52% of the white workforce were in manual jobs compared with 68% of African-Caribbeans and 75% of Bangladeshis. Generally, ethnic minority pay is lower than the majority population.

e The candidate lays out patterns of inequality.

A variety of explanations have been offered for these disadvantages. Cultural explanations try to locate the problem in the cultural character of the minority group. One common aspect of this approach is the claim that minority workers experience communication difficulties. There is some evidence that those that have poorer English do experience difficulty in getting a job. For example, Gray found that language difficulties were a barrier to employment for Asian women in Coventry. However, language is unlikely to be the cause of the disadvantage experienced by that part of the ethnic minority population born in the UK, especially those from the African-Caribbean community.

e This evaluative paragraph examines aspects of the culturalist argument.

It is also argued by culturalists that ethnic minority workers suffer from a skills or qualifications deficit when compared with their white counterparts. However, a large number of studies, particularly Daniel, Brown, Smith etc., have shown that even when the qualifications and experience of ethnic minority applicants for jobs are similar to white applicants, they are still likely to be unemployed or employed in lower job levels. Moreover, there is evidence from experiments conducted by the likes of Brown and the television documentary 'Black and White' of considerable discrimination being practised by white employers against members of ethnic minority groups when it comes to jobs and housing. Studies of education by sociologists such as Mirza, Troyna and Wright also suggest some institutional racism in the education system that may be resulting in African-Caribbean youth in particular leaving the secondary system undereducated and underqualified.

e This section focuses explicitly and evaluatively on the notion that ethnic minority workers may be less well educated or qualified, and appraises that argument confidently by focusing on sociological studies of employer and educational discrimination.

There is not only evidence of direct discrimination against members of ethnic minority groups, but also indirect discrimination. A good example is when dress requirements are imposed which cannot be complied with by members of some groups. Jenkins's research indicates that employers often take into consideration not whether candidates have the right qualifications but whether they are thought likely to 'fit in' to the workplace without causing any trouble. If the employers subscribe to stereotypes about ethnic minority groups, such practices become discriminatory.

e A good attempt is made here to investigate the subtleties of discrimination.

Weberian explanations of ethnic minority inequalities in employment tend to focus on the concept of status inequality. Parkin notes that modern societies are characterised by both class and status inequalities. Power is in the hands of the majority group, making it difficult for minority groups to compete equally for scarce resources such as jobs and housing. This can be illustrated by reference to Barron and Norris's dual labour market theory. This argues that there are two markets for labour — the primary sector, characterised by secure, well-paid jobs with long-term promotion prospects, dominated by white men; and the secondary sector, characterised by low-paid, unskilled and insecure jobs, dominated by women and black people. Ethnic minorities are less likely to gain primary-sector employment because employers may subscribe to racist beliefs about their unsuitability, and even practise discrimination against them either when they apply for jobs or by denying them responsibility and promotion. Moreover, trade unions and a weakly enforced set of laws, e.g. the Race Relations Act, implicitly support this status inequality.

e This is an excellent theoretical section which follows through very logically from the previous section on discrimination.

Some Weberians, especially Rex and Tomlinson, argue that ethnic minority experience of both class and status inequality, especially racism, can lead to poverty. They argue that a black underclass may exist which is marginalised, alienated and frustrated. The left realists, Young and Lea, argue something very similar. They note that young blacks may feel relatively deprived compared with their white counterparts who they can see getting jobs and consumer goods. Moreover, young blacks in inner-city areas feel marginalised, i.e. they feel picked on by agencies such as the police and feel that they have no opportunity to change their situation. Consequently, some sections of the young black population may

turn to criminal behaviour in order to make up for these deficiencies. New Right sociologists, on the other hand, claim that the black underclass is naturally criminal because it has developed a culture of poverty which it transmits to its children. Murray and Marsland blame the culture of African-Caribbeans for their poverty and unemployment in that they claim that young African-Caribbeans, in particular, are workshy and welfare-dependent. However, the evidence does not support the New Right case. Surveys indicate that the norms and values of young African-Caribbeans in regard to work are no different from those of mainstream society.

> 🖉 An excellent section outlines in some detail how status inequality may lead to a black underclass. There is a perceptive link to left realism. The evaluative tone is reinforced by the contrast with the New Right version of underclass theory.

Marxists explain ethnic minority inequalities in employment by reference to capitalism. They argue that black people are part of the exploited working class but they do acknowledge that racism is a powerful ideology which is used by the capitalist class to attain three goals aimed at reinforcing class inequality. First, racism results in black people being denied access to mainstream jobs and having to become part of a reserve army of labour which is used by the capitalist class as a flexible workforce in times of economic expansion and recession. Second, racism by the white working class is not discouraged by the capitalist class because black people are a useful scapegoat when the economy is misfiring, e.g. black people are often accused by racists of 'taking white jobs'. Third, such racism prevents the formation of a unified working class that can challenge ruling class power.

> 🖉 This is a succinct summary of the Marxist position, although it suffers slightly from having no references.

However, it is difficult to prove that racism is a capitalist ideology — it may benefit capitalism in the long term but this is not evidence that it functions exclusively as an ideological apparatus. If racism is of benefit to capitalism, this is probably an accidental by-product rather than a deliberately constructed ideology.

> 🖉 This is appropriate evaluation.

The neo-Marxist Miles argues that we should see ethnic minorities as members of 'racialised class fractions'. This means that they are part of the working class but there are significant cultural differences between them and the white working class. For example, young African-Caribbeans may stress black power to differentiate themselves from young whites through membership of the Rastafarian sect, and there is evidence that young Pakistanis exert their identity through Islam. Other Asian groups may stress family ties and community.

Miles also notes that some ethnic minorities who are members of the middle class may see their interests lying with capitalism, e.g. the Asian emphasis on entrepreneurship, enterprise and mutual support may be advantageous in achieving business success. However, Miles notes that status inequality in the form of racism means that the white middle class will never accept that Asian professionals have the same status as they do.

e This excellent summary of the work of Miles demonstrates that the candidate understands the links between class inequality and status inequality.

In conclusion, then, we can see that the evidence suggests that racism plays a major role in reproducing, maintaining and legitimating inequalities in aspects of employment. The likelihood is that this is not the result of some sort of capitalist conspiracy. Rather, these patterns of inequality are the result of mainly unintentional institutional forms of racism brought about by the failure of social institutions in the UK to adapt to social change, particularly the rapid movement towards a multicultural society.

e This is an excellent evaluative conclusion.

e This candidate has demonstrated a firm grasp of the issues, concepts, theories and debate in regard to employment inequalities. The analysis of theory has been supported with strong evidence, and a balanced, logical and convincing argument has addressed the question thoroughly. The essay has had an evaluative aspect throughout and the candidate has questioned consistently most aspects of the debate. Consequently, this response, although not perfect, meets in all respects what could reasonably be expected at this level. The candidate would therefore be awarded the full 20 marks for knowledge and understanding and the full 24 marks for evaluation, making 44 marks in total.

Total marks: 90/90

Question 5

The underclass

Item A

Charles Murray identifies the emergence of an underclass of poverty in British society. He argues that this subculture is characterised by family instability, violent crime, drug abuse, dropping out of the labour force and irresponsible scrounging off the State. Murray claims that what distinguishes members of the underclass from the rest of society is their refusal to take responsibility for their own welfare by, for example, seriously looking for work when unemployed. Commentators on the left, such as Young and Lea, have also suggested that an underclass exists in UK society. However, there is no attempt by these sociologists to suggest that the character of the underclass is inferior and deviant. Rather, they are seen as being 'innocent' victims of economic and social factors beyond their control, such as global economic recession, government economic and social policies, racism, and class differences as symbolised by differential access to scarce resources.

Item B

Distribution of child poverty, by family type

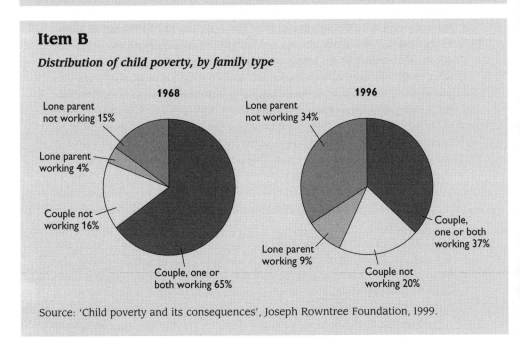

Source: 'Child poverty and its consequences', Joseph Rowntree Foundation, 1999.

(a) **Using only the information in Item A, identify two sociological theories of the underclass.** (6 marks)

(b) **Using Item B, identify two changes that have occurred between 1968 and 1996 in regard to the type of families in which child poverty is mainly found.** (6 marks)

(c) **Identify and explain two problems that sociologists face in researching the existence of an underclass.** (12 marks)

(d) **Using your wider sociological knowledge, outline the evidence for the view that poverty can take a variety of different forms.** (22 marks)

(e) **Outline and assess sociological theories of the underclass.** (44 marks)

Total: 90 marks

Task

This question is for you to try. You should spend some time researching suitable material and making notes, and then try to write the answer in 90 minutes — the time you will be allowed in the examination. Below are a few pointers to help you get on the right track.

(a) You need to demonstrate interpretation skills in answering this question. Read Item A carefully and you will see that two broad theories of underclass are mentioned. Make sure you understand clearly how these differ. Try to put your response into your own words. If you do quote from the item, make sure your quotation is explained.

(b) This question is also testing your interpretation skills. Examine the pie-charts carefully and work out which family types have undergone most change since 1968. Do not make the mistake of just describing the changes — instead, make sure you refer to the scale of the change, i.e. is it a slight or dramatic increase or decrease? Has it doubled or trebled?

(c) Focus on the problems of operationalising the concept. If you examine Item A you will see that sociologists do not actually agree on the social characteristics of the underclass. Therefore, how the concept is operationalised or broken down into measurable form will probably depend on which sociological or ideological position you take. For example, a New Right sociologist is going to ask qualitatively different questions from those asked by sociologists such as Lea and Young. Try to think of the kinds of questions the two opposing schools of thought might ask and how these differ. A second problem is likely to be access to a group that might have the kinds of social characteristics and attitudes associated with an underclass. Think about which social groups are available that might bear some resemblance to a so-called underclass — the long-term unemployed, those on benefits, single teenage mothers — and think carefully about how you might incorporate them into a piece of research. What sort of sampling frame would sociologists use? Is one available? What sampling method is likely to be used? Is it likely to be a random or non-random method?

(d) Poverty can take many different forms. In other words, poverty is not just about lack of income. The experience of material poverty can lead to a diverse range of exclusions. Think about evidence relating to the following:

- the features associated with poverty identified by Townsend or the Breadline Britain survey
- how poverty might impact on family life
- the effect of poverty on educational achievement, e.g. see Smith and Noble, Wedge and Prosser, Halsey
- the effect of poverty on choices in the housing market

- the effect of poverty on health, especially mortality, morbidity and life expectancy
- the effect of poverty on lifestyle, e.g. Graham on smoking, Wilkinson on diet
- the effect of poverty on young people, e.g. Young and Lea's observations about street crime and urban disorder, Craine's study of unemployed youth in Manchester
- the feminisation of poverty

As you can see from the list, there are plenty of areas into which you can dip to show your wider sociological knowledge. Make sure that what you cite is evidence rather than theory and that it is clearly referenced in order to pick up the full marks. Remember, this question is merely asking you to describe the evidence. There is no need to explain why something is the way it is or to evaluate it.

(e) Don't forget that this is an essay question and therefore should be organised as such. Make sure you spend at least 40 minutes on this question.

- Your introduction should define clearly what is meant by the 'underclass', and should 'set the scene' for the debate. You could use Item A briefly to introduce the key arguments and sociologists involved.
- Focus on those theories which see the underclass as a problem. Begin with the culturalist perspective of the New Right thinker Murray. Take each of his arguments in turn, i.e. on parenting, criminal behaviour and the labour market, and summarise them in as much detail as possible.
- Use a couple of paragraphs to show how Murray's ideas are similar to the 'culture of poverty' thesis and Marsland's ideas about welfare dependency.
- Before you move on to examine the alternative structuralist theory of underclass, you will need to spend some time evaluating the specifics of the culturalist position. Take each point you have previously made in turn, e.g. does the evidence support what Murray has said about lone parenting, criminal behaviour and the labour market? What does the evidence tell us about the culture of poverty or welfare dependency? What contribution have empirical studies by Craine or Heath made to this debate?
- Outline the structuralist theory of underclass, stating clearly how it differs from the culturalist position. You will need to analyse the work of Field, Rex and Tomlinson etc.
- Make sure your essay is balanced by including a reasonably detailed evaluation of the structuralist position.
- Try to construct a conclusion which comes down on one side or the other based on your considered evaluation of the sociological evidence available to you, rather than your opinion or the experience of your friends.